PRAISE FOR
DUNCAN CAMPBELL &
THE ART OF BEING THERE

Duncan Campbell's life reads like a kind of human alchemy. He has transformed the pain and loneliness of his own childhood into a system that brings caring and connection into the lives of extremely vulnerable children. His story is a moving reminder of the healing power of relationships and an excellent illustration of the social entrepreneur's journey.

- DAVID BORNSTEIN, Author of *How to Change the World,* and Co-Author, Fixes Column, *The New York Times*

A lot of science says that children who have a consistent, loving adult in their lives are protected from a wide variety of behavioral risks—even when they have a lot of other strikes against them. Friends of the Children is special because it works with the MOST at-risk kids who are often not easy, but who deserve a chance. That's why the mentors need to be paid. This is the story of their journey together with caring, loving adults who have figured that out. We are proud to have supported this model and the research that informs it.

- LAURA LEVITON, Senior Adviser for Evaluation, Robert Wood Johnson Foundation

In my professional life, I've seen only a few programs that I think have a shot at really making a difference. I don't casually toss words around like 'brilliant' and 'unique,' but what Campbell did is brilliant and unique. What he created in Portland could change the way this country tries to help children.

- GARY WALKER, Former President,
Public/Private Ventures

The Art of Being There is a double-treat—the Horatio Alger story of one man's escape from poverty and the account of his long-running campaign to use his business acumen in the service of the next generation. It's a narrative of hope and a prescription for how we can transform the lives of children.
- DAVID L. KIRP, James D. Marver Professor, Goldman School of Public Policy, University of California at Berkeley Contributing Writer, *The New York Times,* Author of *Kids First, Improbable Scholars,* and *The Sandbox Investment*

Friends of the Children is the only program I've seen that is just as rigorous about finding youth facing the toughest challenges as it is in measuring outcomes. This is truly unique – a successful program that insists on serving our country's most vulnerable youth. Duncan has flipped the paradigm on how we use evidence to help these young people achieve success.

- WOODY MCCUTCHEN,
Edna McConnell Clark Foundation

I just find Duncan to be an incredibly inspiring person. He had a vision for building a better world and he is making it happen! When GreenLight was looking for its first proven and badly-needed program to bring to Boston, we found Duncan Campbell and Friends of the Children. We couldn't have made a better choice!

Duncan's life story and life experiences have led him to make a huge positive difference in the world. I am so glad he decided to share these stories and experiences with all of us. Hopefully, this will not fail to inspire all of us to make the same kind of difference in our lives and in the lives of others.

- JOHN SIMON,
Co-founder and Board Chair of the GreenLight Fund
and Co-founder of Friends of the Children-Boston

Duncan Campbell is one of the most caring people I know and he combines that with an astute business mindset, focused on results. Friends of the Children is changing lives and putting these young people on a thriving trajectory.

- ROBERT E. KING, Founder of
the Thrive Foundation for Youth

Duncan, my friend of more than thirty years is what I call a vintage Oregonian. Long before others, Duncan recognized that children have the best opportunity to reach their fullest potential when they have a long-term relationship with a caring adult. That is in fact what Friends is all about. Duncan Campbell has toiled for decades to give these kids a chance to achieve big things. Personally, he is a modest man, but I have seen firsthand how Duncan's quiet style has produced a legacy of powerful, constructive change.

-U.S. SENATOR RON WYDEN

The Art of Being There is a beautiful book at once enormously inspirational and immensely practical, one that weaves together insights from Duncan Campbell's personal journey of purpose, with the story of Friends of the Children's remarkable impact on the lives of young people growing up against the odds. It's chock full of lessons for all of us as individuals, and for our nation as we seek to do right by the next generation.

- MARC FREEDMAN, founder, Encore.org and
Author, *The Kindness of Strangers*

Duncan Campbell's life story is interesting, but his response to his life experience is far more compelling. Friends of the Children provides help and guidance to kids who, like Campbell, might seem to spell only trouble. Friends helps those kids "think bigger" and make truly positive changes. Campbell's dream—helping those kids—helps them dream, helps them fulfill those dreams, and gives them the opportunity and the guidance to write the next promising chapter of their life stories.

- OREGON GOVERNOR TED KULONGOSKI (2003-2011)

In this poignant memoir, Duncan Campbell generously and intelligently shares with readers the moral passion that drove him to a life of service. Through his indomitable and radiant spirit, Campbell transcended a difficult childhood, channelling his love, wisdom, and generosity into an effective program that has touched the lives of many.

- JEAN RHODES
Frank L. Boyden Professor of Psychology,
University of Massachusetts, Boston, and Author,
Stand by me: The risks and rewards of mentoring today's youth

THE ART

OF

BEING THERE

CREATING CHANGE, ONE CHILD AT A TIME

DUNCAN CAMPBELL
as told to Craig Borlase

ampelōn
PUBLISHING

CONTENTS

A NOTE FROM THE AUTHOR

A program unlike any other: Friends of the Children is the solution to breaking the cycle of poverty and thus the intergenerational repetition of low educational attainment, teen parenting, and criminality.

1. We start early: The earlier, the better. We select children at ages 5 and 6, toward the end of kindergarten.

2. Kids facing the hardest challenges: Friends of the Children proactively selects children with the most significant barriers to future success – those facing the highest risks.

3. 12 ½ Year Commitment – No Matter What: We're in it for the long-haul. We stay with each child from kindergarten through graduation, for 12 ½ years, no matter what.

4. Professional Mentors: Each child is paired with a salaried, full-time, highly trained professional mentor that we call a Friend. Friends are paid a living wage and benefits.

5. Unconditional: The 1:1 relationships between Friends and our youth are unconditional. Friends are there no matter what.

Friends of the Children is real, it works and gets real outcomes:
• 83% of our youth graduate from high school or earn a

GED, although 60% have a parent who did not
• 93% avoid the juvenile justice system, although 50% have parents who were incarcerated
• 98% avoid early parenting, although 85% were born to a teen parent

Return on Investment: The Harvard Business School Association of Oregon did a return on investment study and found that for every dollar invested in Friends, there is a return of $7 through reduced social services and increases in tax revenues.

Learn more at: www.friendsofthechildren.org

*This book is dedicated to all of the children
Friends of the Children serves and will serve in the future.*

THE ART
OF
BEING THERE

PROLOGUE

Y ou two are never going to amount to anything," she hissed. "You're just like your crackhead mom. You're stupid and you're going to end up just like her."

Crouched between the cot bed, the crib, and the bunk, she carefully took both her dolls and sat them up against the only section of wall that wasn't hidden by furniture. She smoothed the dress of one doll so it covered the half-chewed leg and rearranged the thinning hair of the other. She slid the small cardboard box she had been saving for days in front of the dolls. *Great,* she thought. *Now they have somewhere to put their beer.*

The tapestry of smells coming from the kitchen was real enough. Gram said there was going to be turkey, mashed potatoes, and all the fixings. *All the fixings.* Those three words triggered the aromas wafting through the already crowded house and led everyone by their noses in the direction of the dinner table. The girl couldn't decide which smell she liked best, but any shortlist had to include the bacon thrown in the skillet before being paired up with the green beans and the ginger that Gram fried in melted butter before adding it to the cranberries.

Nicky stopped and took a deep breath. It was cold outside. It was cold inside too for that matter, but every inhalation of the cool Thanksgiving air warmed her from within. "Today is going to be a good day," she whispered to her dolls.

Of the six Thanksgivings that Nicky had lived through, she hoped this one would be the best. For the first time that she could remember, her family was together. Four generations under the same roof, brought together for the day like every other family in the country. It was a lot to be thankful for.

They hadn't always been together. For a couple of years back, Nicky and her four siblings were in foster care. In the years before that, her mother fought—and lost—daily battles with drugs and alcohol. Even on the notorious streets around their home in Compton, Los Angeles, Nicky and her siblings stood out. As they walked and played and walked some more along sidewalks that were marked by gangs and scarred by violence, the state eventually decided the risks were too great: They took the kids away from Nicky's mom.

Nicky didn't remember the day they left home, and she wasn't there in court to hear her mother beg like a wounded animal to be allowed another chance to clean up and care for her children. She didn't remember much of the two years she spent in foster care either, other than a sense that something vital was missing.

But she remembered the day when her grandmother and great-grandmother Gram stepped in. The two matriarchs mother-henned the five children back out of the foster care system and away from Los Angeles. Together they headed north, at first to a house on the Oregon coast where each night the children fell asleep to the sound of the wind easing its way through the trees. Eventually they settled in a small house in Portland, opposite a grassy park that was ringed by giant cedars.

In time, Nicky's mother followed. But so did her demons.

While the house remained filled with hunger-inducing flavors, something else was happening. Nicky turned away from her dolls and slipped through the bedroom she shared with her two brothers and two sisters. She headed down the stairs, pausing at the sight of her little brother, Logan, struggling upward.

"What is it?" she asked.

Logan let out a noise that was halfway between a grunt and a shout, a guttural noise that only his immediate family could decipher. He'd been this way since birth. Like so many babies exposed to crack while in the womb, Logan was destined to spend the rest of his life dealing with the consequences.

Nicky understood Logan's warning. She paused on the stairs. She heard the front door open. She bent down just far enough to see two pairs of feet crossing the threshold, two pairs of hands depositing four large red, white, and blue boxes on the floor.

Beer, she thought. *And Mom. And Aunt Amy.* She felt her stomach tighten inside. She disappeared back upstairs.

Though she'd just started grade school, Nicky already understood how to deal with her mom: by instinct; knowing how and when to make herself invisible. But her aunt was another story. There were times when, no matter how much Nicky tried to hide, her aunt would go out of her way to hunt her down and attack. She used words, not fists, not physical weapons. And her assault always hit its target, and it always left a wound.

Back in her room, Nicky saw Logan crouched in the corner by the dolls. She joined him as they took turns making them politely eat and drink their way through an imaginary meal. There was no conversation, just silent movements, as they moved their doll's heads down to eat off the cardboard table. But in time both children grew bored of the fantasy. Logan had his doll kick the table over; the game ended.

"Come on down, children," Gram called from the bottom of the stairs. Nicky took Logan by the hand, leading him down toward the source of the magnificent smells, toward the danger of their mother and aunt.

The meal started out well enough, with Gram and Grandma both serving and fussing over their brood. But once Nicky's mom and Aunt Amy decided that food was less important than beer, the atmosphere started to change. Like two boxers circling the center of the ring, each sister tested familiar wounds to see which one was the weakest today.

"Tell me again, why can't you keep a man, sis?" Aunt Amy said, laughing.

"And why is yours not here, hun?" came the reply. "Is he out playing happy families with someone he likes better than you?"

The jabs kept flying as the graveyard of empty beer cans

continued to grow. The food tasted less exciting than Nicky hoped it would, and even though she had barely eaten a thing, she was no longer hungry. Just too much tension to eat. She pushed her plate away. She looked at the silver cans scattered around the table. It felt all too familiar. She remembered the other meals just like this, meals when the weather was colder and there were gifts to be opened, meals that were taken outside to escape the barrage of insults. Whatever the season, whatever the food, the beer cans always took over eventually.

"And what about you two, huh?" Something in her aunt's tone told her she should keep her head down, her eyes locked on the table. But she couldn't resist. She looked up to see Aunt Amy staring back at her. Pointing a beer can at her and her older brother Samuel, she leaned in. A smile like a paper cut was scratched onto her face. It was dangerous to look, dangerous to stare, but Nicky couldn't do anything but keep her eyes locked on her aunt's mouth.

"You two are never going to amount to anything," she spit. "You're just like your crackhead mom. You're stupid and you're going to end up just like her."

Aunt Amy took another mouthful of beer and sat back. Nicky felt her insides turn to stone. She didn't hear much of what came next, the way the words flew faster, how the smiles vanished and the insults increased in volume and spite. If she glanced at her mom, she'd see her face tightening, just as it always had done before she lashed out at the children and left the house for hours on end. Instead, Nicky remained frozen, staring at her plate. The urge to cry was almost too much for her, but if she could be still enough, she hoped she might just win out. She offered up a silent prayer. *God, please make it stop.*

A loud noise brought her back to the room. Her mom stood up, sending the chair backward, and fumbled for the plate that was untouched in front of her, then tried to hurl it at Aunt Amy. A glass hurtled back, missing its target but smashing against the wall.

Nicky didn't wait to be told. The stones inside her vanished, replaced in an instant by fire and wind. She sprang from her chair, picked up her youngest sister from the floor and followed the rest of her siblings out of the door. From behind her came the sound of another plate smashing against the wall, but she was running too fast to worry about it. By the time they made it out on the front step, the shouting from inside diminished a little, replaced by the sound of more furniture thudding to the floor. She didn't stop. None of them did.

Within ten paces they were at the gate. Then they were across the road, the worst noises of home quickly fading beneath the sounds of their feet running over the asphalt. Even though this was the first time they had to escape the house in Portland, Nicky and Samuel knew instinctively what to do. They headed across to the park and made their way to the biggest tree of them all—a giant cedar with branches that hung down low like a ball gown.

Leaving the younger ones playing at the base of the tree, Nicky and Samuel started to climb. Their experience of tree climbing only went back to their arrival in Oregon, but in the few months since they'd arrived, their confidence had grown. Both moved freely and quickly up the branches, arms pulling, legs pushing, chests pressed in close to the timber. Soon the little ones below were all but hidden from view by the mesh of branches they had risen above, but neither Nicky nor her brother spent much time looking down. Instead they kept looking up, to the next foothold, the next limb that would take them one step higher.

As the branches grew a little thinner farther up the tree, so too did the canopy that shielded them from view. They were high up, higher than the roofs of the houses that sat in neat lines around the park. Nicky steadied her nerves and looked up to see Samuel still climbing above. She pushed on, moving slower now, testing each branch more carefully before committing her weight to it. But her progress was steady, and within minutes she was level with Samuel again.

"We should stop here," he said, his back resting against the main trunk, his legs wrapped around a limb. "We're at the thin ones."

Nicky found a branch of her own just below and settled in. She was warm from the climb, and for a time all she did was breathe and gaze out at the view. She'd never been that high before, never seen that far. She'd never felt the branches begin to bend as they do whenever the slightest breeze starts up.

They sat there silent for a long time. Even inside her head, there was a peace and stillness that had settled upon her. She stared down at the street below. Nothing changed, nothing happened. She watched the door of one house open. A family walked to the sidewalk and got into a car. She couldn't see her own house from where she was, but she wondered whether the fight was still raging at home.

The small breeze started up again and reminded her how high they had climbed. She felt a little of the fear that she left at the house creep back inside her. Nicky closed her eyes. *God, she prayed, I can't wait til I'm eighteen and I can leave.*

Even at her age, she knew it was a foolish prayer. But what other hope did she have to cling to?

"What you thinking about?" Samuel asked.

"I don't know," she said. "I think we should go now."

Slowly, carefully, they climbed back down. Logan and the little ones were still quietly playing at the base of the tree, but they seemed happy enough to follow their leaders back to the house.

The living room was cleaned up. The beer cans were gone; the table was pushed back against the wall. There was no sign of Mom or Aunt Amy. There was just Grandma, her back to them as she faced the sink. There was the sight of Gram, her eyes closed and head tipped back, resting in her chair. "Come on," said Grandma. "Let's get you some food."

PART ONE

RISK
&
RESILIENCE

CHAPTER 1

ANOTHER WAY

"No child should have to be raised the way I was."

O f the thirty kids Duncan Campbell saw on his daily
visits to the unit at juvenile hall, Wes was one of his
favorites. He was bright and he was clever. He knew
when to be quiet and respectful when the occasion called for
it, but if the moment was right and life behind bars hadn't
gotten to him too much that day, he could charm you with a
wild smile. He was seventeen, highly articulate and full of
potential. *And,* thought Duncan as he desperately tried to
keep pace with him as they sprinted down narrow back alleys
and across deserted downtown lots, *he's fast, too.*

The day was not going the way Duncan had planned. It
was supposed to be a special time, the sort that boys like Wes
would learn from. It was meant to be a day in which trust was
strengthened and self respect developed, the kind of day on
which this ragtag bunch of law-breaking teenagers might look
back and remember well. They'd remember it all right, but
for all the wrong reasons.

Duncan had been working for the juvenile court for almost two years. It had only taken a few months for the job to feel old, like a pair of new shoes that had started to come away at the sole. For an optimistic, energetic, ambitious man like Duncan, being able to spot the system's fault lines so early was discouraging. Then again, all that optimism, energy, and ambition came with a healthy dose of cynicism from a childhood that had daily served up disappointments and rejections. If anyone was going to see how things could be improved, it was Duncan.

In these cells, bordered by a high fence, there was only one story that was being played out. It was as if boys like Wes suffered an unbreakable magnetic attraction to the justice system. No matter how much progress Duncan thought he'd made through his daily visits, he knew once he'd say goodbye to a boy at the end of his detention period he'd most likely see him again within a few short months in court.

That was the way it was with Wes. He wasn't old enough to graduate high school yet, but he was already an experienced burglar, drug user, and street brawler. He wasn't just locked in a cycle of failed crimes and failed punishments. He was welded to it. And Duncan was going to fix him.

Duncan's plan for helping Wes started with a day out. He made all the arrangements with the swimming pool, got a van, and asked the boys to sign up on the sheet he placed on the canteen wall. It took a few minutes for the slots on the page to fill up, and not much longer for the excitement to spill over into a fight.

On the way downtown, the boys all sat like preschoolers;

their towels and bathing suits rolled up on their laps, their eyes growing ever wider at the streets passing by. Some had only been in detention for a few weeks, yet all of them looked hungrily at the world beyond the glass.

"I've been thinking about an option for you, Wes," said Duncan as he moved to sit in the empty seat next to him.

Wes shifted his gaze from the window to Duncan. "What's that, Mr. C?"

"You should get treatment for the drugs. Fix the drugs, and you fix some of that stupid behavior. Fix the stupid behavior, and you don't have to put up with me for the rest of your life."

Wes smiled. Both of them knew there was little chance that would happen. Worse, once he turned eighteen, if he broke the law, Wes would be tried and sentenced as an adult.

Duncan considered pointing out that there would be no swimming trips in prison, but he thought better of it.

The van pulled up in the parking lot of the pool, and Duncan got out first. His colleagues helped gather the boys and check them off the list for the third time that morning. It was cold and wet outside, and the boys huddled together. As soon as Duncan saw Wes standing some distance apart from the rest of the group, his back half turned to all of them, Duncan knew what was going to happen.

"Don't, Wes," he said. "Please."

Wes looked back. "I'm sorry, Mr. C," he said. And then he ran.

Duncan had always been an athlete. He didn't hesitate to run after Wes. Short and quick, he was better at short distances, but he still had some game. He had been both line-backer and quarterback on his high school football team. But that was well over a decade ago. As Duncan turned the first corner, he could feel the gap widening. By the time he saw Wes turn down an alley midway along the second block, he could feel his lungs burn. Once Wes cleared the parking lot at the back, Duncan was done. In a race between one person running for his freedom and another racing for his pride, the outcome was predictable.

Duncan walked back to the van, his chest heaving. He'd lost Wes in three blocks, but he knew that wasn't the whole story. The truth was that he had lost Wes a lot further back than that. More like three years. *Or was it?* When did a kid like Wes become out of reach? When did he slip so far through the cracks that there was no getting him out? Was it before he even started high school? How early would Duncan have had to catch Wes to have really made a difference in his life?

Duncan had an innate fascination with questions like these, just as long as they didn't remain rhetorical. The last thing he was interested in was navel gazing and pontificating. What he cared about were results. After all, his own life had taught him that change was possible, that people could change, rise above their circumstances. How could he help others?

It was that simple equation that had led him in the first place to take on a position as childcare worker in the juvenile detention home. It was a good job; it blended well with his studies in law school. But having seen kids like Wes return to the unit again and again, Duncan grew doubtful that the

Juvenile Justice System was able to permanently change lives for the better.

By the time he reached the bus, the rest of the kids had been taken in to the pool. Duncan didn't feel much like swimming, so he sat and watched from the side. He thought about an article he'd read once detailing the seven behaviors of the adult children of alcoholics. Somewhere on that list were the words *too trusting*. If the description hadn't resonated with him then, it certainly did now. He had trusted Wes, not just with the offer of a day out at the pool, but with something far bigger. Duncan had believed he might have been able to influence Wes to change the trajectory of his life by making better decisions. Duncan had made himself vulnerable, believed that with enough time, enough consistent support and honest conversations, things might have begun to turn around for his friend. Instead he was left feeling betrayed.

Duncan looked out at the remaining seven boys as they thrashed around in the pool. Many of them couldn't swim— not that it seemed to limit the amount of fun they were having—but it struck him as sad all the same. Things could easily have been different for them if only they'd had someone with the time and the few cents it would have cost to take them swimming when they were young. Now, unless they made a bold choice and decided to learn to swim as an adult, they were destined to be held back by fear in the shallow end.

Were any of his colleagues going to get in the pool and help out? He doubted it. Like him, they probably believed it was too late to make a difference. But unlike his colleagues, Duncan wasn't going to quit trying. In the two years he had been working with young offenders, Duncan had concluded that many of his coworkers thought of the job as just another civil service position. Either that or they saw the children as terminal failures.

While Duncan shared their frustration, he refused to sign up to their defeatism. He believed there had to be a better way. But what?

***

NOT THAT LONG AFTER THE TRIP to the swimming pool, Duncan moved on. It wasn't a choice motivated by cynicism and it wasn't at the request of senior management. He left the unit for something far more mundane. He left for money. Once back at law school, he worked hard to earn his degree and become a lawyer, and after that he went to work for Arthur Andersen, an accounting firm.

A year or two in, Duncan became a Certified Public Accountant (CPA). After three years, he was ready to make a change. While most people who had a childhood like Duncan's would have thought they'd died and gone to heaven to have become successful as both a lawyer and as a CPA, Duncan's heart wasn't in it.

"I'm an entrepreneur, not an accountant," Duncan told his boss as he placed a handwritten envelope on the man's desk. "It's how I'm wired. If you're a middle-class kid with connections, there's always someone who can help out; a family favor to pull in to help you get ahead in business. But when you come from poverty like I did, there's no one around who can give you any money. Whatever you need, you have to earn for yourself. When it came to selling donuts for the school basketball team, I sold more than anybody else. Why? Because that was my best option for making enough extra money to buy the tennis shoes I needed. Kids like me grow up with initiative in our veins, and you can't just expect us to fit in with a big corporation like worker bees in a hive."

His boss just stared back.

"That's why I'm resigning," Duncan added.

After a little more staring, his manager decided it would be a mistake to let him go. They sent him to Hong Kong for six months, then gave him a special job working out solutions for their clients' most complicated tax problems. They made him a manager; they gave him an office. They trained him some more, and put him to work for clients who were at the cutting edge of their business.

But it only put a temporary stop on the path toward the inevitable, and within a few more years Duncan was standing in front of a different partner, sitting behind a bigger desk, in a nicer office, trying to explain that he was feeling bored again.

"How about I have a sabbatical?" he asked.

"Sure," came the reply. "You can be an accountant for any firm you like, just so long as you don't do charity work—only accounting work."

Duncan thought for a moment. Charity work was exactly what he had in mind. So he moved on to plan B and pulled out the envelope from his pocket.

"In that case, I'd better resign."

What next? Take on a job as director of social services? That wasn't an altogether terrible notion. He was already working hard within the juvenile justice sector. Though he had left juvenile hall some years previously, he had been approached in the past by county officials looking for a new and more effective way to allocate money to children's services. They formed a Juvenile Services Commission, and Duncan, given his law background and juvenile hall work, was asked to join the commission, later becoming the commission's chairman.

But, much as it was in his days spent chasing kids like Wes around the block, he grew impatient. The pace of change wasn't quick enough. The kids' lives were deteriorating quicker than the prevention work could kick in. Instead of playing politics and worrying about how this decision or that initiative would go down with the voters, he wanted to be a genuine catalyst for meaningful, more active, and faster change.

Maybe it was the fact that he was a father by now, or maybe it was just what happens when a person hits his early thirties and realizes many of his dreams are within reach. Whatever the cause, his childhood no longer saddened him. He had done enough crying and agonizing about it. It was time to let it go—not deny it—but to move on.

He remained a passionate advocate for the kids that reminded him of himself: the "Little Duncans". In spite of everything that had gone wrong for him as a child, there was enough that went right; kind words and encouragement from his friends' fathers and brothers, the football coach, and his own older brother. They had all been there in ways his

THE ART OF BEING THERE| 33

parents—now dead—had not. Juvenile services commissions were all well and good, but by now he was convinced that it was next to impossible to change people fifteen years old and over. Unless they had a transformative event or access to great resources, the recidivism rate was alarmingly high. The only ones who stopped were the ones who had the herculean strength to be able to choose it for themselves.

In a way, realizing this set Duncan free from full-time social services work. Not that he didn't care—he cared about the Little Duncans more than ever—but in seeing the system's inability to propagate lasting change, he freed himself from the burden of having to throw his lot into it. Instead, he decided to embrace his inner entrepreneur.

Option A was to start a national pizza chain. It was a good enough idea, but with a young family at home, the idea of so much travel didn't seem like the best fit. Option B was to apply the knowledge he'd gained from his recent work at Arthur Andersen to forest products companies making lumber and plywood, setting up a timber investment firm. Given that nobody was investing in timber at the time, option B was far and away the biggest risk. Naturally it was the one Duncan took.

And so began Campbell Global.

The business plan was simple. First, convince forest products companies that instead of keeping the land on which they were growing their timber, they would be far wiser to sell it to the Campbell Group (Campbell Global's original name before it was later changed). Second, work out how to grow and harvest timber in a more efficient way. And third, find people with money who were willing to invest. It was a simple enough idea, plus nobody else was doing it. So, Duncan hit the phones.

Working through his list of major investment funds, he added cold call salesman to his previous job titles of lawyer and CPA.

"Hello," he'd say a hundred times a day, "this is Duncan Campbell, president of Campbell Global, a timber investment firm. I'm going to be in your city soon, and I would like to meet to discuss timber as an investment."

"No."

"No."

"No."

Some people can't handle the level of rejection Duncan had received. But he'd been hearing the word no all his life. He was used to it. He had grown callouses and blisters in all the right places, so it didn't leave him sore or weak. *Instead,* he told himself, *all I need is one yes.*

Just one.

In between the phone calls and the rejections, Duncan would often take a moment to move out from behind his desk and look out his window. The office wasn't extravagant or expensive. It didn't need to be for a business with six employees, no clients, and an ever-expanding list of creditors. But the office did have one thing going for it—a view of Northeast Portland across the Willamette River. He'd look at the gray skies sitting heavy over the streets he had grown up on as a child, and repeat to himself two of his favorite mantras:

Campbells don't quit.

No child should have to be raised the way I was.

CHAPTER 2

HAPPINESS, A FICKLE FRIEND

*"It was a hollow form of happiness...like a piece of fruit
on which the skin looks good enough, but
the flesh is rotten through."*

he room looked bigger when he woke up. The street-
light that shone through the thin curtain sent eerie
shadows of monsters and dragons across the floor.
Through his open door, the darkness in the space beyond
held even more fear than usual. Duncan listened. There was
no sound, not even the usual noises that creaked throughout
the house at night.

He decided to run to the safety of his parents' bed. Head
down, arms out, he walked quickly from his room and into
theirs, his three-year-old eyes refusing to give in to the temptation to try to see what terrors were waiting in the darkness
that sat like fog at the bottom of the stairs. *Just keep walking,*
he told himself. *Just keep walking.*

His parents' bed was empty. Their smell was in the room,
and their clothes were scattered about the place as usual. But

they were not there. Duncan paused. He was thirsty now, and confused, too. Where were they? Where had they gone? Why were they not in bed? He struggled to breathe as the reality of the moment hit him hard, stunning him. In the darkness, he realized he was alone—and afraid.

Head down. Eyes fixed. Arms at the ready to defend himself, Duncan edged back to his room. He made it back and turned on the light, but he felt no better. He needed to find them. That was all he knew.

His pants still felt warm and familiar as he picked them up from the floor, but they were no comfort as he struggled to force his legs into them. He had been able to get himself dressed for at least a year, but doing it under the influence of so much fear turned his fingers to ice and his legs to stone.

Eventually, his pants on inside out, he was ready to search the rest of the house. With the lights on, he searched the two rooms but only discovered what he knew already was true: Nobody was there. He was all alone. The fear of monsters and dragons and other terrors of the night had gone now. In their place there was something worse. All he could feel now was an ache inside his stomach, a hollow feeling that had a curious painful edge to it. His parents had gone. He had to find them. Without them, he was lost.

There was no noise on the street outside. Duncan couldn't find any people or any lights on in any of the houses. What few cars there were in the neighborhood were all parked for the night, and the buses had long since stopped their day's work. He edged down the front path, used both his hands to pull back the heavy gate, and stood on the sidewalk watching.

To the right was the park, but instinct led Duncan to walk left, toward the main street. He watched his bare feet as they moved across the ground, soaked in the orange wash of the streetlights.

"Kid, what are you doing out here?"

Duncan looked up to see a man dressed in white looking back at him. There were lights on inside the shop behind him, and the smell of freshly baked bread warmed the air. "What are you doing, son?" said the man again.

"I'm looking for my mommy and daddy," said Duncan, doing something no three-year-old should have to do. "They're not in their bed."

The man crouched down and put a hand on Duncan's shoulder. He smelled more of tobacco than bread. "In that case," he said, "we'd better find them."

Today, Duncan is unsure about what followed next. At some point he was eating warm bread, feeling his stomach relax with every mouthful he swallowed. There was a policeman who took his hand as they walked back along the street. And there was a door that opened onto a tavern in which the lights were so bright that they hurt Duncan's eyes. And there were his parents, sitting on bar stools. They smelled of tobacco, too, but not warm bread. Everything that they said was too loud for Duncan. He just wanted to go back to bed.

Duncan's childhood was measured out in bar stools. When he was three he could climb down from one of them by himself. When he was five he could get up on top of one of them without help. By the time he was seven he was tall enough to lay his head on a scarred wooden countertop, and stare down the line at the glasses and bottles that receded into the distance.

After his parents left him alone at night the first time, they left him alone again and again. It seemed perfectly normal to them that a couple would head to the bar for a few hours on a weekend, leaving a kid like Duncan at home. Sure, he cried a bit when they got him home that first time, but what harm could it do?

The Campbell house was not abusive in the strictly physical sense of the word. His mother was kind, but she was over-whelmed. She worked hard as secretary to an equipment sales firm. Though she wasn't much for yelling, she wasn't physically affectionate, either. Like his father, she was never violent when she drank, but she was neglectful. She put her own felt need for the numbing medication of alcohol above the needs of anyone else in her life. She was self-absorbed to the point of ignorance.

His father was more complicated. He never revealed any of himself to his son, never shared any of his secrets with his only child. He was private, never speaking about his time as a navy diver during World War II, never talking about his own childhood, never sharing anything other than the bare essentials about which place they were going to go drink at that day.

Aside from giving him a place to sleep and food to eat, the Campbells did nothing for Duncan. They knew nothing about how their son thought, nothing about the nightmares that tore through his sleep, or the fantasies that fueled his days. They had no idea he was a gifted athlete and a fine student. They were physically present to the bare minimum of requirements, but emotionally both of them had permanently left the building.

Life followed a simple routine in the Campbell house. His mom worked hard during the week, holding down a job. Permanent employment, however, was a puzzle that his father never quite managed to solve. Any work he did manage to come by—mostly driving heavy construction equipment—would never last more than a few months. And when he lost his license for being convicted of too many DUIs, life got even harder. About the only thing that he had going for him was a semi-entrepreneurial streak that reemerged with the winter snows each year, inspiring him to spend a few hard weeks shoveling snow for local businesses. As the snows melted, so too did his ambition.

If his parents had money, they would drink bourbon and vodka. If not, they would drink beer. During the week they restrained themselves a little, but by the time Friday came around they were unable to resist the urge to hurl themselves into alcoholic oblivion at the nearest bar.

Duncan quickly grew accustomed to doing things on his own. Each Saturday they would either give him twenty-five cents to go get pancakes for breakfast or let him join them in the bar of a Chinese restaurant, where he would eat chicken noodle soup and fried ham sandwiches while they drank. On Sundays he'd get up early and leave, his parents sleeping off the excesses of the night before. He'd go to church alone, come home and find them still in bed, still filling air with their stale odors. By the time the evening came around, he would tune in to *The Ed Sullivan Show, The Whistler, The Jack Benny Show* and *Mr. and Mrs. North,* the sound of his laughter echoing throughout the house.

Duncan's only respite from the grind at home came either from school or from long summer vacations, during which he lived with his grandparents for weeks at a time. When he returned home from the endless days of home-cooked food, playing cards, and the blissful hours spent helping with chores around the house, Duncan was welcomed by the all too familiar dread feeling that nothing had changed. Often, it was worse than that. He'd find strangers in the house, men who'd met his parents at bars and needed a place to stay.

At times Duncan had to share his room with these strangers, and like his parents, they too had trouble with alcohol. They'd wake him up when they crashed into the room late at night, their mumbling and groaning going on all the while as they searched for their cigarettes and matches. Often, they would fall asleep while smoking, and Duncan grew accustomed to the shouts that would follow the moment these drunken strangers realized their mattress was on fire.

Yet one night a drunk passed out in his room didn't wake up immediately. Duncan awoke to the confusion of heat and smoke that was filling the room. Unable to get past the mattress that was now buried beneath flames as tall as Duncan, he was saved only when a passing cab driver saw the smoke pouring out of the open window, heard Duncan's shouts, and smashed the glass so that he could rescue the boy. Fortunately, everyone made it out alive.

Even when life was calm and relatively uneventful, something was missing. His parents never helped their son with his homework, they never went to see him play on the football team. When he was eight Duncan wanted to be a Cub

Scout. It was no problem for him to find the meetings and get himself to them, but in order to be sworn in, every cub was required to have a parent present at the ceremony. Duncan had told his parents over and over again when and where the ceremony would take place, but he wasn't at all surprised when he looked out across the hall before the service started and couldn't see their faces. During the whole program he kept looking around, but neither of them showed up. As the evening finally drew to a close, the cub leader quietly knelt down next to Duncan as he sat, head down, on the front row. "I'm sorry," he said.

The evening ended with the newly sworn-in cubs running down the aisle to meet their happy parents. Duncan remained where he had been the entire evening, staring at the floor, watching his feet swinging violently back and forth. Once enough time had passed and most people had left, he would get up and head home.

"It's okay, son!" came a booming voice from the back of the hall, accompanied by the sound of a row of chairs being bowled over. "Duncan! I made it!"

Duncan looked around. His father, drunker than a skunk, staggered in at the back of the room. His arms were spread wide, his face flushed with color. He was wearing a smile that was arrogantly unaware of the pain he had caused, as well as the further embarrassment he was inflicting on his son with every passing second. "You can still get sworn in, lil' Dunc. Your old dad didn't let you down!"

Duncan's body tightened. He summoned every ounce of strength that was within him and marched down the aisle, pushing by his pathetic excuse for a father and out toward the night air. Once he was clear of the building he started to run. He sped along sidewalks and down alleyways. He ran past gas stations where men with bow ties pumped gas into cars weighed down with happy college students. He ran past the tavern from which his father must have stumbled, and to which he would surely soon be returning. He ran down his street, through the gate, only stopping when he reached his bed. And there, as he had done on so many other nights, he cried until the tears stopped and sleep took over.

His parents never told him they loved him. They never asked how he was doing at school. They hardly knew the names of any of his friends, much less any of his tormentors. They knew little about his teachers, nothing about his success, and nothing about his struggles. They never told him when to go to bed, they never told him to pack up the jigsaw puzzle and get a good night's sleep because tomorrow was a big day. They never told him that they were a little disappointed in the way he had behaved during the day and wanted him to try better. They never sat on the edge of the bed to read him a book or ask him what he thought. They just ignored him. To Mr. and Mrs. Campbell, it was as if this little person who looked like them, shared their last name, and lived in their house was just a shadow. To them, Duncan was almost a ghost.

From an early age, Duncan Campbell knew he was alone in the world. He knew that his parents were indifferent. Whether he succeeded in life or failed, it would make no difference to them at all.

So Duncan—even before he reached double digits—

became not just the man of the house, but the mother, too. Every year, on a Saturday just after Thanksgiving, he'd wander the empty house and take whatever he could from his parents' pockets, drawers, and wallets. He'd take whatever he could find, sometimes three, four, or even five dollars, and as soon as he determined that he'd had enough, he'd leave the house and head out into the cold. He'd pick out a Christmas tree from a lot down the street. Even at a young age he was a discerning customer, carefully assessing the trees from every angle. He only liked the bushy ones, and would often ask the guy selling them to cut the top one-third off, so that it would look even bigger.

Duncan was strong, the undisputed sit-up champion of the school, so he could drag the tree home easily. Once he had done that, he'd get out the stand and the ornaments from the cupboard. He'd rearrange the furniture in the living room so that the tree could occupy its usual place in the corner. Over the course of the afternoon he would add the decorations, carefully placing each one in just the right place. It was a difficult job, one that required patience and skill, but the end result was always spectacular: a tree that appeared to be so full of life it might just walk out of the room by itself.

Duncan always loved the moment when he could stand back from the tree, and for the first time admire his work. But he hated it, too. It took only seconds for the thrill to turn to sadness as, yet again, he had done on his own something any normal family would have carried out together.

Every year, often hours after he had finished the tree and the sky outside was run through with darkness, Duncan heard his parents stumbling onto the porch and struggling through the door. Sometimes they would cheer at the sight of the tree, other times they would make no mention until they got another drink in them. Invariably, one of them would eventually call Duncan to come from his room. "It's Christmas!" they'd say, as if this was news to him. "We should celebrate!" And with that they would stagger back out the door and lead him to the Chinese restaurant, where they fed him pork chow mein and ordered themselves just a couple more beers or whisky sours. Finally, when they'd had too much to drink and had forgotten that their son was sitting with them, Duncan always slid out from the booth and walked home alone.

The tree always looked beautiful when he walked in. The sense of pride at having chosen and set it up so well always warmed his heart. But it was a hollow form of happiness. It was like a piece of fruit of which the skin looks good enough, but of which the flesh is rotten through.

Every year as Christmas approached, that hollow feeling only got worse. In Duncan's mind, every other child in the world was standing in front of their Christmas tree, thrilling at the sight of the gifts piling up beneath it. All Duncan could see were the bare floorboards and the sawn-off base of the tree wedged into the stand. Sure, he could put up the tree and make it look nice, but someone else had to provide the gifts. And they never did.

And so Duncan learned that happiness was a fickle friend. Happiness could never last for Duncan. Happiness was never strong enough.

CHAPTER 3

A GLIMMER OF HOPE

*"He says one day they'll take me
to the juvenile detention center."*

If there was a soundtrack to Duncan's first two or three decades, it could only contain songs by Motown greats like Smokey Robinson and Marvin Gaye. His peers might pick Elvis Presley or James Taylor, Otis Redding, or Springsteen, but none of them would fit well enough. None of them could match that same sense of joy and pain, that same hope and yearning that cracks through Smokey's falsetto or Marvin's range.

The close proximity of joy and pain became a familiar theme for Duncan. From Christmas trees to Cub Scout initiation ceremonies, events that were meant to be happy affairs were easily soured. Even something as innocent as having a friend home from school was dangerous, as Duncan found out early on in the fifth grade. Duncan had brought a friend back home, and at first it all went well. The two boys were playing cards at the kitchen table when a noise from outside turned Duncan to stone.

Seconds later, the door smashed open and his father collapsed within the boundaries of its frame. From his mouth came a hurricane of shouts, mainly indecipherable words hurled at no one in particular. His friend froze, too, staring at a sight he'd never seen before. How could this volatile and angry man actually be a father? How could it even be possible?

"Let's go," said Duncan, pulling at his friend's arm. "Now." He led him downstairs, carefully closing the door behind them. Beneath them the shouts carried on, which the two boys tried their best to ignore. Duncan was already finely tuned in to his father's moods: like a storm watcher, he knew the warning signs. Much of the time when he was drunk, his father would lie in a heap and shout at the air. Occasionally he would pick up the phone, put in a call to some distant relative on the other side of the country, and shout down the line at the bemused recipient.

Duncan's face flushed with embarrassment as they played. All his friend had ever seen was the side of himself he presented at school: funny, spirited, occasionally a wise guy with a mouth that got him into trouble. Though he was never tall in comparison to the other boys in his class, Duncan's personality always managed to take up more space in the classroom or playground than others. But not now. Not at home, with this wretched man shouting and cursing and most likely soiling himself downstairs. The shame was almost unbearable. Almost—Duncan knew he could not give in to his emotions. He needed to keep his wits about him. The winds might change at any point.

It didn't take long for it to happen. The shouting ceased,

and Duncan pulled back from the card game. He moved to the door, opening it just a crack. While his friend couldn't translate the low rumbles and slurred speech, Duncan knew exactly what he was hearing. He stood, eyes staring into the middle distance, his ear halfway through the door.

Quickly, he pulled back and shut the door. His voice was different; urgent, panicked. "We gotta go now," he said. "My dad just called the cops on us."

The two boys hurried out of the house, too fast for his dad to respond, and hid around the corner. Duncan's friend spoke first. "Why would your dad do that, Dunc?"

"He's always threatening to call them and tell them that I'm…" Duncan paused as he tried to remember the word his dad had used the last time they argued. It was a strange word, one he'd never heard before. He had looked it up that night as he sat in his room. What was it again? "Incorrigible."

His friend looked confused. "It means he thinks I'll never change," explained Duncan. Silence settled on the two boys again as they watched. Soon a police car arrived, and an officer disappeared into the house.

Duncan looked away. "He says one day they'll take me to the juvenile detention center."

His friend kept his eyes on the house. "Do you wanna stay at my house tonight?" he asked.

His father continued to drink and act cruelly, so Duncan chose to spend as many days and nights as he could in other people's homes. He rarely brought friends home, and on the few occasions that he did, it was only those whom he trusted most, the sort who might understand the kind of mess he came from. One friend was an African-American boy who moved to Portland from the Deep South to join Duncan's fifth grade class. They had a shared love of baseball, but more importantly, a shared sense of being outside the party. When Duncan invited him to lunch at his house, his new friend's first response was, "What are your parents going to say when they find out I was there?"

Duncan grew to understand that his life was different from others. On the occasions that he went to his friends' houses he always returned home feeling as though he was stepping back into a darker world, where even the sun failed to shine as brightly. He grew accustomed to the fact that his house was never filled with the smells of home cooking; that it was more likely to be dominated by the shouts of drunken strangers than the strains of music or laughter. He was white trash, the kind of outsider whose family friends resolved feuds by shooting one another, the kind of kid whose mom cut the telephone wire with a pair of scissors when she saw the size of the phone bill accrued by her drunken husband (thanks to his long-distance prank calls). Duncan was the kind of kid who was destined to fail.

Somewhere inside him, there was a voice that fully agreed with that prognosis. But it was not the only voice he listened to, because when he was twelve, Duncan declared to himself that he would never grow up to be anything like either of his parents. So, with an angel on one shoulder and a devil on the other, Duncan entered his teenage years, making a good start at school, becoming a conscientious student who dedicated himself to his studies. Eventually, however, he began to drift.

It was his temper that started it. It frequently landed him in the principal's office, and he was suspended twice for fighting in high school. Sometimes it wasn't the anger that landed him in trouble; instead it was simply a desire to be noticed. Like the time when a student pontificating from the stage during a class election assembly tried to make a joke in front of the whole school. The gag fell as flat as a lead balloon, and in the silence Duncan let out a fake laugh that sounded like a braying donkey. The whole school thought it was funny, which gave Duncan the temporary high he craved. Yet when he got an essay back from a teacher the next week, with a fat letter D scrawled in red ink across the top, he was incensed. Duncan only ever got As and Bs at school. He had never earned a C, let alone a D.

"How did I get a grade like this?" he asked his teacher. "Hee. Hee. Hee," came the teacher's reply, perfectly mimicking Duncan's own forced laughter from the previous week.

As soon as the class was over, Duncan barged his way down the hall. A kid threw an apple away, missing the trash can by accident and rolling into Duncan's path. He picked it up and hurled it back. Unfortunately, it landed square on the chest of a senior. At the sight of the scowling little kid standing defiantly in the hall, the senior's friends crowded around. "You're not going to let him get away with that, are you?"

With a shout of, "You little punk," the bigger boy marched over to Duncan, but before he could start his attack, Duncan unloaded on him. The fight was broken up within a few seconds. Duncan was never going to let fear get the better of him.

What Duncan's teachers didn't realize was that his behavior grew out of the circumstances of his home life. While they tried to deal with the symptoms—that mouth and those fists—they missed any chance of truly helping him. They had no idea how much better it was to change the circumstances of a child like Duncan rather than to deal only with the behavior. They treated symptoms rather than causes.

Together with his friends, Duncan formed a half-baked gang, which set up a half-baked shoplifting ring. The plan was simple: lift things from a downtown department store and return the items to the same store for cash. It was only a matter of time before they were caught, and when it happened, the parents were told to come and get their kids from the local police station.

His mom's face was tense and red when she walked through the doors and saw him, head hung low, slumped alone on one of the benches in the police station.

"I'm supposed to be at work," she snarled at him as they walked out. "I had to miss my shift at the hotel." Apart from visits to the principal's office, it was the only time Duncan could remember that one of his parents had interrupted any of their plans to be with him.

Things deteriorated at home. His family lost the house. They had to move into an apartment nearby. He noticed his parents starting to search through his dresser drawers, looking for quarters to buy beer. The neighborhood taverns began kicking them out, refusing service.

When he was older, he learned to dread the sound of the front door opening. It always meant his parents were back.

He'd hear them bumping into the furniture, which was always followed by yelling bouts and the sound of his mom phoning the police. On more than one occasion, the cops showed up to tell his parents to knock it off or someone was going to jail.

Eventually one of them did, though not because of the violence that accompanied their constant drinking. His father was desperate for money, and had begun writing bad checks. As crimes went, it was ill conceived and poorly executed. However, the prison term was equally ineffective, doing nothing to change him. Once he was out, he continued with the bad checks. What changed was his drinking. Four-day sessions became more common, and he'd only return when he ran out of money or good will at the tavern. He'd show up one morning, equal parts surly and repentant. Duncan knew to stay far away.

Father and son only ever had one conversation about the older man's drinking, which came toward the end of his life. "Why did you do it?" Duncan asked.

"You'll understand some day," he said, his face twisted with venom and self-loathing. "You'll understand why."

"No," said Duncan. "I don't think I ever will."

Not everything about the declining Campbell family fortunes was bad. Moving to the apartment meant new neighbors, plus the discovery that pretty much any parent was capable of doing a better job raising a child than Duncan's parents. The father of one of his new friends even took both boys fishing one morning. It wasn't the first time Duncan had been taken out for the day, but on the few occasions he had made a trip with his own parents, it was usually a picnic organized by one of the dive bars that typically ended with Duncan stealing away to avoid the drunken arguments that ensued. This quiet fishing trip was nothing of that sort.

There were others who showed an interest in Duncan as well. He started meeting the older brothers of his friends, boys who looked out for the younger ones. One high school counselor even pulled him aside one day, kneeling down close to his chair. "You know what, Duncan," he said, "you've got potential. You just need to slow down and focus. And don't let the anger take over."

It was enough to tempt him into dropping the goofball act and starting to work hard in all aspects of life. He had always been dedicated to his homework, turning the radio on as he studied alone at night. He even took dancing lessons, found he had talent, and finished second on *High Time,* Portland's star-studded equivalent of *American Bandstand.*

Bit by bit, Duncan could see some version of a future beginning to appear in his imagination. It was vague, and for a while all he really knew was that wherever it took him his future would be played out far, far away from Portland. To get there, he had to find his own path. And that meant work. So, starting as young as ten, he made sure he always had a job. First he was a caddie, hitchhiking the six miles, round trip, to the golf course. He found a job as a boat boy at the yacht club. With it came a dream of one day owning a boat.

To get there, he knew he would also have to deal with his behavior. That was simple enough, and once he decided he was not going to be like his parents, he turned his back on his bad friends, put his punk ways behind him, and embraced his desire to excel. When he wasn't earning money or studying, he would play ball all day, feeding his insatiable desire to get better. He found competition everywhere he looked: elections for class president, end of term tests, even the line to get lunch in the school cafeteria. If someone else was trying to succeed, Duncan wanted to get there before him.

By the time he started his sophomore year in high school, his father was back in prison and Duncan was taking care of himself without any help. He earned his own money and cooked his own meals. He gradually began to realize something that would change his life forever—what he had been through already in his young life would have been enough to crush others. A different kid exposed to the same level of alcohol-induced neglect might well have turned to drugs or alcohol himself. Another kid might have given up hope, he might have believed he was about as worthless as his parents' behavior suggested he was.

But not Duncan. He had discovered something vital about himself: that he liked people. He rarely had enemies and he rarely fell out with people. He kept a part of himself private, protecting the core of his identity, but every other part of him was an open book. He was a natural extrovert who believed that most people were kinder and nicer than his parents. He was a natural scholar who understood that if he worked hard enough, he would eventually succeed. He was a natural survivor whose inner resilience had already brought him through a series of difficult trials. He was yet to make anything of himself, but he already knew that he could be someone of consequence.

In his senior year, Duncan was the starting linebacker on the football team that won the city championship. At the heart of the team was a coach who believed in him. Coach didn't rescue him or give him money or take him from his house. Instead, he gave him something far more important: a belief in himself. He offered affirmation and encouragement. Duncan had no idea how profoundly powerful those two ingredients were. To a child like Duncan, an adult who is consistently present and consistently encouraging can wipe away the deleterious effects of years of neglect.

Therefore, when a high school counselor told Duncan that he had the ability to do anything he wanted in life, he had no reason to doubt it. The only problem was in deciding what he should aim at. Should he be a doctor? A lawyer? Why not just throw his passion behind becoming a millionaire? He couldn't decide, but he did at least know that all of the above would require him to go to college. The lack of money was a problem, but he even had a solution to that. Duncan ran an ad in *The Oregonian*.

Wanted: private loan for young man
putting himself through college.

He didn't get any replies, but it didn't crush him. Why would it? He'd already grown accustomed to people ignoring him. Sooner or later he would find success. So he worked harder than ever: at a car rental agency, as a dishwasher, as a gas pump attendant.

He was alone, just as he always had been. Unlike those early days of wandering the streets with his pants inside out desperately searching for his parents—unlike all the times he wished his father would vanish entirely—by the time Duncan was applying to college, he felt liberated by his parents' lack of interest. He wasn't so much alone as he was free.

CHAPTER 4

CHASING A DREAM

"Dealing with the symptoms rather than causes, relying on deterrents, believing that incarceration would automatically lead to rehabilitation...there had to be a better way, didn't there?"

The room was full of people his own age, but somehow every single one of them bore the air of adult maturity, the kind of poise that only a real man could carry off. For months, Duncan had watched and listened, noticing their elegant penmanship and their easy talk of five-figure salaries. Next to these students who were the same age as him, Duncan felt like a child.

Throughout the year, he had chosen to act the way he had as a child, lifting his head, clenching his jaw and setting his eyes to their most charming sparkle—while working three jobs. He was determined to be a success at the University of Oregon law school. There was no other option.

Daily he repeated his self-created family motto, that Campbells don't quit. He knew all the evidence presented by the lives of his parents suggested that Campbells really did quit, that they really did bail on their responsibilities, that they really did lack the kind of drive and ambition to which Duncan so aspired, but that wasn't the point. Campbells don't quit was more of a statement of intent than a verdict on past performances. More than that, it was a simple prayer of petition. Campbells don't quit.

The bigger truth was that he already had quit. He started at Oregon State University, but by his junior year he left and got himself accepted at the University of Oregon School of Law. It was there that he faced the daily challenges springing from his feeling out of place. Not that feeling out of place was anything new.

What really bothered him was the fact that the study of law didn't match up to his expectations. Duncan wasn't the first student to dream of being a great courtroom attorney like Perry Mason, and he wasn't the first to discover that law had less to do with fighting injustice and defending the innocent than he hoped. He wasn't the first to grow bored of the study of law for business and personal injury. But the disconnect bothered him all the same. To Duncan, the law really did seem like the best tool for social transformation, the best chance at making people's lives better. According to his class, however, winning mattered more than the pursuit of justice. It created an atmosphere Duncan didn't like, and so, after a year he switched, joining the business school.

While he quit on the law degree, he didn't quit on himself. Duncan added three more mantras to his collection, forming a handful of sayings that he called The Campbell Creed:

Campbells don't quit. Campbells don't complain about a problem, they fix it. Campbells aren't phony and never try to be something they're not. And, finally, Campbells always show love.

After graduating in 1966, Duncan hitchhiked across the United States and Europe, working along the way and seeing a world far different from that of Northeast Portland, which was all he'd known as a child. Until his epic road trip, he'd never even left Oregon, and the endless supply of new people offering new perspectives on life stimulated his appetite for spending time with people.

He returned to Portland full of confidence. His Oregon degree didn't quite have the same prestige as a similar degree from an Ivy League school, yet when Duncan saw there was an opportunity to work for a prestigious Fortune 500 company, such as Boise Cascade, he refused to concede any reason why they should not offer him a position.

Dear Sir,

I am an alumnus of the University of Oregon, graduating last summer with a degree in business. I believe I am equal to any graduate student from Stanford or Harvard. I am bright, resourceful, and hard working.

I would therefore be most grateful if you would consider my enclosed application.

Sincerely yours,
Duncan Campbell

The letter worked. Within weeks he had moved to the company's head office in Boise, Idaho, where he supervised the construction of some condos for the company in Sun Valley. Within months, however, he was bored of the work and disillusioned by the discrimination he witnessed, and had returned to Portland. He wanted to be fulfilled. Nothing less would do.

Duncan started working for the juvenile court. He was happy to finally be about the business of what he really wanted to do—working with kids who suffered childhoods like his own—and he was amazed that there were people who were willing to pay him to do so. Yet it only took a couple of years for him to see that too little change was happening in the kids, a fact which continued to bother him as he made a final attempt at a law degree. Somehow he was able to silence the old doubts about whether he truly belonged alongside all those other would-be lawyers who came from wealth and privilege. And because Campbells don't quit, Duncan graduated. Arthur Andersen beckoned, as did the opportunity to become a CPA. The first quarter of his working life was complete.

And so it was that Duncan Campbell's inner entrepreneur found himself at the start of the biggest adventure of his life. Staring out of the window of the offices rented by Campbell Global, he looked across the Willamette River, back toward the neighborhood that had provided the background for his childhood. He had come a long way, that was clear, but the challenge that lay ahead of him was far greater than any he had encountered so far.

Campbell Global started in 1983, with debt. With no collateral to his name, Duncan put on a suit and tie and engaged in an interview with his bank to assess his moral standing. These were the last days of the so-called character loans: opportunities for upstanding citizens to gain a bank manager's trust and confidence and—eventually—tap them for a loan.

He spoke about his plan to buy 160 acres of land in Northwest Oregon and subdivide and sell those units for $25,000 each to doctors and lawyers and any other wealthy people he could find. It was an untested and risky concept. The idea was so new that Duncan, surprised, left the bank with a $25,000 loan and a line of credit at four times that amount. He was in business.

Not everyone agreed with his plan. A trusted friend, whom Duncan respected as a business leader, laid it all out on the line when Duncan asked for his advice.

"You want my advice? Are you crazy? You're never going to find anyone who's going to invest in timber. You're never going to find anyone who will sell you any land. The whole idea is nuts."

It wasn't enough to put Duncan off. Instead, it spurred him on. Having already majored in finance, become a lawyer, and developed a working knowledge of the realities of the forest products industry, he was convinced that the collection of his experiences was enough to see him through.

He purchased the land he'd been looking at for $2 million, with a $20,000 down payment, and set about cold calling potential investors. It was hard work, but the enthusiasm coming from the knowledge that he was doing something brand new, with so much potential, kept the small staff team on board. Aside from Duncan there were a forester, two salesmen, an assistant and Duncan's wife Cindy, the company's part-time Chief Financial Officer.

Accountants who work for companies that make no money at all have an interesting job. And when they happen to be married to the owner and have firsthand knowledge of just how precarious the finances have become, the pressure only increases.

"We can't keep doing this," Cindy said, more than once.

Each time, Duncan offered the same reply, delivered with a smile, a shrug, and a brief pause before moving on to the next phone call. "It's all going to work out in the end."

Those early days were marked by the distinct absence of money. Having moved from their first house and invested in a couple of apartment complexes, Duncan and Cindy had leveraged themselves to the point where there was no more financing available. It fell to Cindy to keep track of the notes and loans and property tax statements for all these properties, warning Duncan of how desperate things were getting when they didn't make mortgage payments or pay property taxes for a whole year.

"It's a hard way to go to bed at night, Duncan," she said. "I'm just hoping you know what you're doing."

Duncan remained calm. The first years passed, and while they were making a few sales, it was only ever enough to cover costs already incurred. Even though no real money had been made, that didn't worry him so much. They ran out of money, having used up all their credit with the bank, but again, Duncan refused to panic. He asked friends and family for help by acting as guarantors of further bank loans. He cut costs further by making sure that whenever he and a colleague traveled, they shared a $79 room. He listened to a friend tell him that at his age, even if things went wrong, he could still build a life from scratch again.

Again they ran out of money. Once more Duncan was forced to beg and borrow from anyone who was willing to take a chance on the business. However, with monthly wages going out and bills piling up, it wasn't long before they ran out of money again. And again. And again.

Many times Cindy told Duncan there simply was not enough money in the bank to make payroll, and each time Duncan did what he had learned to do as a child. He went out and fixed it, secure in the belief that one day his plan would work.

Duncan became convinced that if there was a route to success, it was made up of small steps. If he spent a little more and employed only knowledgeable, high performing people, he would stand a better chance of making things work. He believed that most employers cut corners and went for lower staff costs, but that this lack of quality would show up in the medium and long term. He made sure that he and the team watched every penny, that they became knowledgeable about negotiations and contracts, and that they put systems in place that would allow for quality analysis.

The team dedicated themselves to learning how to get the best timber from their land. They became known as leaders in best practices for forestry, winning environmental awards and helping to pioneer new techniques in stream maintenance.

In their fourth year, they ran out of money for a sixth time. Somehow, in defiance of all logic, they managed to secure a last-minute loan from the bank. The staff threw a party to celebrate. Someone put some music on. Duncan smiled as the drums and strings struck up the first bars. It was his favorite song. Couples formed, and they shimmied their way around the desks as Smokey's falsetto rang out across the office. *Mistakes? Maybe,* he thought. *Crying? Not here. Not now.*

There was no way he was giving up. He'd keep on trying, keep on pushing. If Campbell Global failed, then so be it. But *he* would never quit because Campbells don't quit.

Besides, by now it wasn't just about the money. Success meant more to Duncan than knowing he had obtained whatever financial goals he had set for himself. Success in business was vital, but it wasn't the end of the story.

Looking out across the river, he saw the place where his own life had begun. He thought of the kids just like him, the Little Duncans, the ones who needed help. They were struggling, dealing with things that no kid should have to deal with, but if they could just get a hand up, if they could just get someone to help them, then life could be different. Why couldn't he use his life experiences and his resources to help kids escape, just like he had?

All the time he had been working on the business—even back when he was with Arthur Andersen—he had been volunteering his time with the Juvenile Services Commission. He sat through meeting after meeting, advising as best he could how the commission could make a difference in the lives of the kinds of kids who ended up on the juvenile justice treadmill.

He had no clear answers, but he did have a sense that something was radically wrong with the current system. Dealing with symptoms rather than causes, relying on deterrents, believing incarceration would automatically lead to rehabilitation—these ideas belonged to another century. There had to be a better way, didn't there?

So, with profits still eluding him but with an even greater sense of purpose, Duncan threw himself into Campbell Global with even greater passion. He made more calls, took more flights, identified the pension and endowment fund managers who were the key investors he wanted to work with. Like an athlete in off-season training, he pushed himself harder than ever before. When rejection came, he gave himself even less recovery time. He focused more clearly on the prize, refusing to give in.

"Duncan," Cindy said one evening, when the last of the employees had left, but then she paused. She looked troubled, more than at any point during the previous five years. "We're not doing well. This time is not like the other times. We've got enough money for one more month, then there's nothing. Only this time, I can't see how anyone's going to lend us any more money."

Duncan took a breath to speak, but there were no words. There was nothing to say. In a silent corner of his mind he heard Smokey sing once again. He couldn't give up hope.

He sat back down at his desk, pulled out his call sheet again, and picked up the phone.

CHAPTER 5

THE BALTIMORE SECRET

"This was his calling. This was his mission."

Duncan sat back in his chair and stopped listening. This was one tedious meeting. It had been that way since it had started thirteen minutes ago. There was little chance that would change. On either side of him sat men in suits throwing questions out into the air, disinterested in the answers they received. Duncan looked back at the paper in front of him, on which he had scratched absentminded notes alongside his agenda. At the top of the page, next to the words Juvenile Services Commission, he drew a large question mark.

Duncan was impatient for change, especially now that he had seen what happened when hard work paid off. When success finally landed on Campbell Global, it landed in full and without equivocation. At some point in the early years, Duncan had put in a call to one of the big financial services companies, hoping to persuade them to invest. While they were reluctant at first—preferring to begin work with the startup by paying them a commission to purchase a couple of large properties on their behalf—eventually they suggested a formal business partnership.

Working with a major player in the business world meant that doors previously shut were now suddenly open. It was as if, overnight, Campbell Global had become decades older, with a reputation that went before them. Companies with household names and major pension funds were listening, willing to make deals, and before long Duncan and his team of spirited risk takers were celebrating their first major investment, worth $25 million.

Most businesses similar to Campbell Global don't last more than a year, especially when they have created a product that has not previously been seen on the market. Yet somehow the company had managed to hold on. For five years they managed, refusing to give in, unwilling to give up. And once that first deal was struck, the numbers only went one way: up. The next investment was a staggering $200 million, and more was to come. Success had finally landed.

For Duncan, the money was nice, but it wasn't the end of the matter. He had not lost his desire to help others. In many ways his own success had intensified his desire to help others as, bit by bit, he began to wonder: might all this money he was making—as well as all this experience he was gaining—actually make a difference?

Sitting in the low ceilinged room of the Juvenile Services Commission, it was hard to see how change could manifest. Yet on the day he sat doodling while his colleagues filled the air with empty noise, something happened. He met Orin Bolstad.

Orin was a clinical child psychologist who, like Duncan, had put himself through college by working at the local juvenile detention facility. And just like Duncan, his experiences there had convinced him that the system was offering too little, too late to the teenagers it locked up.

Orin had come before the Juvenile Services Commission in the hope of securing funding for a project he was pursuing through his work as director of the Morrison Center, a non-profit that worked with children who had been exposed to adversity and trauma. While the other members of the commission wanted to talk about gangs (the latest hot political topic of the day), Duncan leaned in, looking hard at Orin.

Throughout his life, there had always been something unique about Duncan's smile. His mouth was always half turned up at the corners, as if it was on a perpetual hair trigger, just waiting to break into a full on beaming smile. People were drawn to him through it, finding it engaging, welcoming and perfectly natural—not forced. His eyes, though, told a different story. They were dark, the iris almost blending into the pupil, giving him the sense that he was somehow taking in more than other people are. Together, that easy smile and probing stare told the deeper story of the mind firing behind them.

Once Orin finished his pitch, Duncan waited for the other members of the commission to finish asking all their questions. He had his own burning questions that demanded to be answered.

"That's great, Dr. Bolstad," Duncan said, "but is it going

to work? How are you going to focus what you do to make sure you get results?"

The ensuing conversation between Duncan and Orin lasted longer than the commission's meeting allowed. The two men went on talking, first in the hall, then over lunch. They talked about past experiences working in juvenile detention centers and about the problems of treating youth crime as a political—rather than a social—issue. Both men soon discovered that the other was equally impatient with the pace of change. Both men wanted to see action and results.

"It's all too little, too late," Duncan sighed.

Orin paused. "There are two guys named Spivak and Shure[1] who wrote about this. They're saying it's around age five or six when kids are starting to go wrong. That's when we as human beings begin to make wrong choices about how we deal with problems. Juvenile court gets to them a decade too late."

Duncan agreed. He knew that it was hard to make a quantifiable difference to teenagers' lives, but was the system really missing the window of opportunity by that much?

"You know," said Orin as the lunch drew to a close, "there's a guy out in St. Louis who's doing wonderful work with kindergarteners. He's getting them to amicably resolve conflict. It wouldn't be out of the question for us to raise some private money and run our own pilot program to see for ourselves if his idea works."

---

[1] Shure, M.B. & Spivack, G. (1982). "Interpersonal Problem-Solving in Young Children: A Cognitive Approach to Prevention." *American Journal of Community Psychology,* 10, 341-356.

"How much?"

Orin shrugged; it was self-consciously nonchalant. "Twenty-five thousand dollars."

Duncan didn't blink, instead agreeing to help fund a pilot program and see where it went. It turned out to be the start of a long and significant friendship. Orin and Duncan combined forces to launch the first project. Orin oversaw the clinical side of things, making sure there was a small control group. They worked together with a kindergarten class at a school in Duncan's old neighborhood. After the trial was over the results were clear: with a little bit of guidance, kids as young as five or six really could learn how to navigate their way through conflicts.

Two more projects followed, each man refining his work. Each time the results reinforced their shared belief that if anyone was serious about tackling the problems of youth offenders, they were going to need to start young.

By the time Campbell Global started to make money, Duncan and Orin's conversations had moved on as well. What had begun as a discovery of their mutual dissatisfaction with the status quo had developed into a passionate belief that there were practical solutions to big social problems.

"So much of this comes from the work of Michael Rutter," Orin said over one of their monthly lunches. Rutter was Orin's mentor, and was widely recognized as one of the leading researchers in child psychopathology. "I studied under him in England. I learned about how he had studied the riskiest kids, exploring how they built resilience. He found out that for many young children, their being exposed to a certain amount of difficulty—a certain degree of risk—was like being given a live attenuated vaccine. Just as the body builds up natural defenses to cope with the viral attack, so also the struggling child learns to cope. Risk and resilience. That's what so much of it comes down to."

Duncan's food lay untouched in front of him. He thought back to his own childhood. There had been plenty of risk. These weren't just the threats of burning houses or being left to wander the streets alone at night when he was too young even to go to school. There was monumental emotional risk as well; the risk of being embarrassed in a hall full of friends, the constant risk of continuous rejection, and at the hands of the two people who were supposed to have loved him more than anyone.

He remembered the nights when, lying in his bed in the darkness, he would slow his breathing, making it as shallow and as quiet as he possibly could. He wanted to be able to hear the very first sounds his parents made if they were to approach. He wanted to be ready when they crashed in through the door. Though the fear was often raging within, he taught himself to stay quiet and not cry out. He learned the hard way that drawing attention to himself was never a good idea.

He remembered how he made himself quiet and still at the kitchen table, his homework spread before him on a weekend afternoon, his father slumped in the corner and shaking off the final moments of an alcoholic sleep. He knew how to watch him, to track his father with his peripheral vision. He knew how to monitor his stirrings, and he understood precisely when it had become time to leave the house and escape to safety.

He remembered countless times when he would look up from his lap as he sat in a tavern to see his parents laughing and shouting, singing and dancing with each other. They never laughed or sang with him, no matter how hard he tried to encourage it. But perhaps if he could just perform well enough, other people might take notice.

Though Duncan was aware of his parents' failings, he did not feel sorry for himself. Did he feel grateful for the circumstances that had helped him develop this resilience? Maybe that was going a bit far. Even so, he was in his early forties, married with three children and already a lawyer, a CPA, and a millionaire. Something must have gone right. And even though he didn't want any child to suffer his childhood, Duncan was thankful to God for the way his life was working out.

Both Duncan and Orin were invited to take part in a series of meetings through which the organizers hoped to synthesize ways to reorganize state governance for children. On the drives to and from the state capital, they continued their conversations about Rutter, about resilience, and how it was that Duncan had managed to survive his past without succumbing to the rut that had swallowed his parents.

There was also a good deal of bitching about the meetings themselves, most of it coming from Duncan.

"I hate meetings," he said as they left Salem and headed north to Portland. "They're so boring. They never accomplish anything. This is the last time I'm going." He always blew off steam like this. Orin would always listen politely and smile.

One day, however, he caught Orin off guard. "What would it take for you to leave the Morrison Center and come work for me?" Duncan asked. "We could do some good together."

Orin scoffed. "You're crazy. Why would I do something like that? Are you kidding me? I've got a great board of directors; they love me, I love them. Why would I leave?"

Months went by. The same meetings took place, and Duncan followed the same script, slumped in the car on the way home.

"You know," he said one day, when he grew bored hearing himself repeat the same lines about how poorly managed the system was and how unlikely it was that it would ever get better, "I was serious about hiring you to work with me. We could develop something that could really make a difference. We could start an institute; we could scour the country for the most successful projects. You could travel all over to find what you like, then come back and tell me how we might implement it here in Portland."

Orin had been at the Morrison Center for fifteen years, and he was feeling an itch. Even so, leaving would require a colossal leap of faith. "The idea intrigues me," he said. "But it scares me, too. I wish I could get to a kid earlier in his life, but to do so we'd have to build something of substance. It would have to go further than just two guys talking about it in a car. We'd need staff, and a budget, and a commitment to the long haul."

Duncan shrugged. "Fine," he said. "None of that fazes

me. I'll happily pledge money for three years to get an institution started."

Leaving an established, respected clinical center was a risk, especially when it was to start something entirely new and untested with a guy who made money selling trees. Yet Orin knew Duncan well enough to be satisfied that together, their combined experiences and skills had considerable potential. As a businessman and entrepreneur, Duncan was well known in powerful circles. Helping children overcome adversity wasn't something in which Duncan dabbled to make himself feel important. It was personal. Thanks to his background, Duncan was determined to make it work, and he was willing to put up the money to prove it.

Neither of them wanted to set up just any old program, and both knew that it would take time to think about what was needed. It wasn't just Duncan's money he was putting on the table, it was his passion. Together, those two ingredients went a long way in keeping Orin engaged.

"Sure," Orin said. "Why the hell not?"

Orin and Duncan set up the Campbell Children's Institute and, just as planned, Orin took off around the country looking at various other programs. It was an exciting time, a period where the days felt as though they were flooded with optimism and potential. Sure, the politicians were stuck in their search for solutions, but all over the country there were nonprofits and community groups, academics, and private individuals tackling the problems that weighed down the lives of so many young people.

When Orin returned from a trip to Minnesota he couldn't

stop talking about the quality of the work he'd seen there. "It's the most creative place for children, Duncan. You've got all these big corporations—3M, General Mills, Northwest, American Airlines—and their staff didn't feel right driving their Mercedes through all these impoverished neighborhoods on their way to work. They felt bad, they wanted to know what they could do, so they all got together and started investing in projects that are making a proven difference."

Of all the places and the people Orin visited, he admitted that none excited him quite like a mentoring project he'd found in Baltimore. A friend at a nearby foundation was so impressed with it that she had started volunteering there herself. It was simple—just spending time with young kids at risk of falling through the cracks, teaching them to read, being a positive influence in their lives—but all the evidence suggested that it was working.

"Duncan," Orin said as soon as he got back, "you've got to come and see this."

A few weeks later the two men made the flight east. They met a mentor who left them speechless. He told them that he was a member of the local community, that he didn't have a college degree. He volunteered his time free of charge. Others in the neighborhood saw him as a leader, someone who had long been a consistently positive influence on their children, whether through tutoring or coaching sports.

As a mentor, he was able to do even more, though he was clear about the limitations and the secret to any future success. "The problem is time," he said. "These kids are so troubled, so seriously risky. I'm mentoring fifteen of them. If I could get down to mentoring just eight of them, and be paid to do it, things would be different."

The flight back was something else. Orin and Duncan giggled like school kids, toasting each other and high fiving their way home. Housed in one spoken sentence, from one conversation, taken from one afternoon visit, they had come face to face with a plan that shone out at them with more power than a sky full of suns.

Orin was on a roll. "Anyone who does risk and resilience work knows that mentoring works well, but there are inherent problems. It's hard to get long-term quality mentors who will commit to a project when they're not being paid. But this—"

"—This is a plan!" said Duncan.

"I've had eighteen years of experience working with some pretty disturbed children," Orin said. "I see them for an hour a week in therapy. These kids live in areas with gunshots sounding off all around them, where Mom's doing crack and Dad's in jail. When they're up against all that, you're not going to change a kid with one hour of psychotherapy each week."

While Orin carried on talking, Duncan disappeared into his thoughts. He wanted to start right away, to find mentors and pay them to work with children who were at-risk. Why? Because finally it was clear to him: He was put here to do this. This was his calling. This was his mission.

A few days after they returned home, the two men took a day to reflect on things at one of Orin's favorite retreats which was owned by the Episcopalian church. They spent their time walking, talking, and thinking through their plan. Midway through the afternoon an office window opened, and a kind looking man with thinning hair leaned out. "What are you guys doing? I want to know."

Duncan followed Orin into the Bishop's office. They sat and told him all about their idea, starting with their sense that the Juvenile Justice System was going about everything the wrong way. They talked about risk and resilience, about wanting to find the kids who were in danger but who, with the right kind of help, could be encouraged to thrive. When they'd finished talking, the Bishop spread his hands, smiled and told them that the best thing he could suggest was that he pray.

"Only you, Lord, know why you've gathered these two men together," he said. "And I pray that your will be done."

CHAPTER 6

FORMING THE FOUNDATION

"Something too many kids were missing: a friend."

The Bishop's words mattered. While Duncan and Orin brought to the table considerable experience and expertise, both men were aware that what they wanted to do was profoundly unique. The Bishop's words gave their confidence a vital boost. Perhaps this wasn't merely a good idea; perhaps this really was a calling.

The encouragement they received added to their hunch that they were heading in the right direction, and not just because of what they had seen in Baltimore. Having worked in mental health for eighteen years, it was obvious to Orin which direction the tide was flowing. Almost every new policy initiative was underpinned by the same drive: to serve more kids for less money. The biennial budget cut was nearly always accompanied by a directive to cut operational costs, while simultaneously increasing service impact.

Duncan and Orin wanted to do something different from almost every other service. They wanted to spend more money on fewer kids. They wanted to invest heavily in a few, to find the highest-risk kids and build in them the one factor that would allow them not just to avoid crime but to construct a life of fulfilled potential. They wanted to build resilience, even though resilience didn't come cheaply.

Both men knew—one through observation, the other through personal experience—that some kids were born with the smarts required if they were to rise above their circumstances. These were the Little Duncans, and they were the original focus of Duncan's work. Compassion for kids just like him had already led Duncan to plough $300,000 of his own money into a fund he called Youth Resources. The money was there to help any kid living in poverty gain access to the kind of activities that were traditionally the purview of the middle class. This included everything from music and dance lessons to summer camps.

Not every child had the kind of drive Duncan had. Some needed more than a taste of success, more than a small spark to set the tinder alight. As Orin and Duncan talked, Duncan began to see that it had taken very little support and encouragement for him to find his way out. So what about the ones who didn't have the same innate drive and resourcefulness? Could they make it out, too?

Orin had spent the best part of his previous eighteen years searching for an answer to that question. He was convinced kids could make it out of a difficult childhood in one piece, provided they had someone in their lives able to be a consistent, positive influence. Over the years he had worked with kids who demonstrated positive results because of all manner of transformative relationships—kindly neighbors, tireless teachers, long-suffering uncles. All of them had the potential to provide a child with the kind of platform upon which they could build a better life than what waited for most of their peers.

"I think we should take a small group of kids and give them a ton of services," Duncan said to Orin as they drove away from their time with the Bishop.

"Can you imagine anyone ever buying into an idea like that?" Orin said.

It was a conversation often had in those early months. Even though they always recalled the traditional arguments on why mentoring wouldn't work, they could never get away from what they had seen in Baltimore.

Through further discussion with the project managers in Baltimore, it became clear that Duncan and Orin could put in place some vital principles early on in their work. First, it was clear that while volunteers could be devoted, they rarely had enough of the time that was required to be able to offer real, tangible support to a child. One hour a week just wasn't going to cut it. Instead, high-risk kids needed about four hours, across each week, with their mentors.

Second was the matter of what a mentor should be doing with the child. While some schemes focused on sports or homework, both Duncan and Orin were convinced that their mentors should focus on relationships. They should hang out, talk, build trust, allow a genuine friendship to develop. They weren't interested in providing at-risk kids with another substitute social worker, parent, or teacher. What they wanted to provide was something too many kids were missing: a friend, the kind who—like a loving aunt or uncle—would look out for them, take care of them when needed, and act with the child's best interests at heart.

Working out of an office in the heart of Duncan's old neighborhood, the two men covered the walls with maps of Portland's streets. They gathered the latest statistics they could find for child abuse, poverty, and crime rates, annotating the maps with them. A clear picture then emerged. Northeast Portland emerged as the winner in the race to the bottom.

Having figured out which were the riskiest neighborhoods, the next steps were clear: identify the schools, get approval from the school system leaders, find some mentors, and then find some kids. Many professionals in the city knew Orin and could vouch for him, and Duncan's philanthropy—which included the purchase of an old house in the neighborhood in which he'd grown up—demonstrated that he was serious about his intentions. The house was put to work as a study center for children, and because Duncan's childhood friends' houses were safe, fun places to be, it became known as the Friends House.

Other benefactors with deep pockets could have simply written a check, but even though he had written plenty of those in the past, Duncan was motivated well beyond what would have been considered normal. Starting his work with Orin was an emotional decision, driven by a desire that other children might not have to suffer through the same childhood that he'd had to endure. It was a practical decision, too, having worked in the Juvenile Justice System for so long. He had become convinced that life could have been profoundly different for the kids he'd seen if they'd had a genuine, wise, supportive friend helping to guide them toward a better path. Finally, it was an empirical decision, thanks to the research that told Duncan and Orin it was entirely possible to create resilience in children if a relationship was forged over a long period of time with an adult role model who instilled positive values in them.

There was one last reason. Duncan had the satisfaction of watching Campbell Global thrive like never before. If ever Duncan felt as though he had been put on earth for a purpose and had been given the financial resources to make that mission work, it was now.

Much of his time was spent at the offices of Campbell Global. These were rooms full of people, full of life. But the office in which Orin and his assistant worked had some magnetic pull on Duncan: Like a fresh pad of paper, like a forest that had just been planted, these rooms were quiet but no less full of potential. Duncan liked spending time there, and he visited as often as he could.

Between the walls covered by their annotated maps, the two men put the finishing touches on their plan. They knew that by employing mentors rather than relying on volunteers they would be able to attract—and retain—the very best for the job. What to pay them? Being a mentor was going to be real work, the kind that made a real difference in the lives of children, so why not pay them the equivalent of a high school teacher?

They also knew that they had to get their ratios right.

Parole officers served at a ratio of 1:50, while the average caseload for social workers was in excess of 100 kids. At the Morrison Center each caseworker saw thirty children, yet Duncan and Orin proposed that each of their mentors cap their involvements at just eight. It was unheard of. It was expensive, too. Both men knew they would be criticized for spending so much money on so few kids.

But their response was simple. At that time, it cost the state about $45,000[2] to send one child to the juvenile home for one year, which, incidentally, was about the same amount it would cost if they sent that same child to Harvard for the same length of time. Duncan and Orin wanted to recruit children from the toughest schools in the toughest areas, the ones who troubled even first grade teachers. These were the children of crack addicts, of serial offenders. They were living in poverty, they faced a bleak future. These were the kids who would end up in the Juvenile Justice System. They were doomed to wreak chaos on society, and they would cost the taxpayer a small fortune.

For less than the price of locking one of them up for a year, Duncan and Orin wanted to invest heavily in the lives of eight such kids. They wanted to build lasting, positive relationships, to be something too many kids had never really had before: a caring adult who was also their friend.

If they could save just one kid from a life of crime and punishment, they would be able to justify the expenditure. Save two, and the community would be significantly better off.

It was bold thinking, and it went against the grain, which

---

[2] Today, depending on the state, that figure ranges from $65,000 to $100,000

was precisely the motivation that drove them the hardest. For most people, straying away from the pack prompts fear and hesitation. Campbells don't quit, not even in a situation most people would have avoided in the first place.

"You know," Orin said, sitting at his desk one morning as he and Duncan made plans for how they could start a pilot program, "if you really believe in this model, you can't just fund it for a short time. Three months of mentoring isn't going to make enough of a difference in these kids' lives, and neither will six. If you're serious, Duncan, you've got to commit to running the pilot all the way to the end. You've got to fund it for all twelve years."

Duncan paused. "You're right. Draw up some figures and let me know how much it's going to cost."

Before he left that day, Orin placed a single sheet of paper on Duncan's desk. It detailed the salary costs for three mentors over twelve years, plus a small budget for expenses and office costs. It was a lot of money. It was also a figure that held the potential to transform the lives of twenty-four of some of the most at-risk kids in the city. It could be twenty-four fewer people in prison, twenty-four fewer people in gangs, twenty-four fewer young parents who were only just adolescents themselves. It could be the redemption of twenty-four lives nobody thought could ever be anything other than a train wreck. It was a lot of money.

The next morning was bright, the kind of midsummer morning that throws out the heat early and refuses to let up. It was the kind of day in which the temptation to give up and leave early is strongest.

Orin walked into Duncan's office. There, front and center, Duncan made a personal commitment to give a couple of million dollars so that they could launch Friends of the Children.

He glanced up at Orin with a smile and said, "Let's go find some salaried, professional mentors for these children. We'll call these mentors *Friends.*"

PART TWO

PLANTING SEEDS
IN
PORTLAND

CHAPTER 7

HELPING KING'S KIDS

"Duncan Campbell? I thought you were dead."

Duncan sat in his Mercedes outside King Elementary School, allowing himself a moment's pause. So much of his past had been played out on the other side of these tall doors. He remembered times when he had acted out, doing precisely the kinds of things anyone would expect of a bright young child from a home characterized by neglect. He winced as he remembered how he would push his way down the corridors between lessons, desperate to win the race to be the first to the next destination—a race that most of the time he was the only one aware of. He recalled what it felt like to make a whole class laugh, and a teacher frown in disapproval.

These were not his only memories, however. There were others that made him feel calm, peaceful, and still. There were kind teachers who told him he had potential, and good friends who stood by him. Most of all, he remembered that every time he arrived at King and saw those doors standing like

89

giant castle gates, he relaxed. School was safe in a way home was not.

Forty years on, the doors looked a little smaller. This time Duncan was about to enter the school as a stranger, but more than ever before, he needed the staff to trust him. He needed them to give him a break.

As he stood in the heat that overtook the school while the kids were out on summer vacation, he wondered what his chances of success were. He had heard that the school had a new administrator, that it had gone through some tough times and was hoping to improve. Would the new principal be one of the old guard, entrenched in the system, weighed down by bureaucracy? Perhaps he would be timid, fearful of jeopardizing his own position so early in his incumbency. There was always a chance that he might be just like the staff Duncan had met at the juvenile facility, the kind who frequently cast blame for personal failings and rarely offer innovative ideas to fix a broken system. If he met with any of the above, Duncan was in trouble.

The idea of doing something to help children who were at risk had been growing within Duncan for decades, and the early conversations with Orin had helped to bring the dream into focus. Yet once the two men had decided how they were going to work things, Duncan discovered that he needed someone to help him put the plan into action.

For that, he turned to long-term friend and educator, Mike Forzley. Mike's background in juvenile court and in Portland's public schools made him an ideal choice for Duncan's first managing director. He didn't just know the communities and the schools they were served by, he knew how to work alongside teachers, gaining their trust and harnessing their expertise.

Mike suggested three schools to approach with the idea of becoming involved in their pilot scheme for Friends of the Children. All the schools were tough, but King Elementary beat the others hands down. It was the worst-performing school in the worst-performing district. There was no better place to start.

Duncan got out of his car, pocketed the keys, and walked inside. The halls were empty, and even if he had needed directions to the principal's office there was no one around to offer any help. Still, Duncan knew precisely where he was going. He walked into the bright outer office. Of all the cold calls he had ever made, hardly any had ever been in person. But this one was special.

Having introduced himself and asked to see the boss, he sat and hoped for a good response. Within less than a minute the office door opened and a tall, middle-aged, bemused looking African-American man emerged.

"You're Duncan Campbell?" he said. "I thought you were dead."

It was Duncan's turn to appear confused.

The Principal explained that after he came to King he was handing out annual student scholarship awards. "Every year there was one award that stood out; the Duncan Campbell Award. I've been in education for thirty years, and I've never seen an award that made such a difference as that one. I still run into parents who remember their child winning that award, and all of them talk about how it changed their child's life. All this time I had assumed you were just some do-gooder who had left money in his will to help students."

He was right in some ways. Duncan had set up the award years before, giving $1,000 and a plaque to the student who had overcome the worst odds. Even though the award was given to middle school pupils, they didn't get the money until they graduated from high school. It was another of his attempts to help the Little Duncans, to encourage them and inspire others to persevere in the face of adversity.

"I'm glad it has helped," Duncan said. "But I want to talk to you about doing something even better."

The Principal introduced himself as Joseph Malone and invited Duncan into his office to talk. Duncan gave the short version of his life's story before moving on to explaining the theory behind Friends of the Children, and how he wanted to implement it at King. He told him that he wanted to find all eight children for one of his Friends right there at King.

Joseph looked at Duncan. "It's changed a lot since you were here. We have serious issues with student achievement," he said. "We have 819 pupils here. Most of them are African-American, living in poverty. Their parents struggle against the threat of gangs, drugs, and all kinds of other troubles. We're even providing school buses so students don't have to walk three blocks to school. It's on the verge of a disaster, but I believe I can make a difference here. The truth is, there's nowhere to go but up. So, yes, Duncan Campbell, I believe in what you're doing. And I'll do whatever it takes to support you."

Joseph was born and raised in the South. He was one of eleven children. Like him, his father had been a teacher and high school principal, while his mother stayed at home. When he heard Duncan speak of the important role that adult friends could play in a child's life, Joseph remembered the long list of people who, along with his parents, had helped raise him. There were aunts, a pastor, and plenty of neighbors who all had helped shape him.

The concept of Friends of the Children seemed to resonate with Joseph immediately. Instinct and experience—both from his own childhood and his time as an educator—told him that what Duncan was proposing had the potential to work. He liked the fact that it was a chance to positively influence kids at an early age. To him it was obvious that Duncan's proposal was a gift to the school, to the families, and ultimately to the children. As an educator, he knew intimately what teachers dealt with when they encountered children who needed help.

Joseph knew well enough that, while a teacher can educate a student in the fundamentals like reading and writing, what they could not do was synthesize hope or provide familial guidance. Children moved up a grade each year, teachers switched to different schools, families broke apart or struggled through colossal burdens. The educational system was not equipped to offer the truly empathetic help many of the children at King needed.

While Joseph knew a lot of people liked to say they were going to change the world (but never actually did), he felt like Duncan wasn't simply grandstanding when it came to how he talked about making a difference. Instead of reciting statistics or trumpeting his achievements, Duncan simply came across as a person who cared about others, the kind of guy who would happily keep on giving $1,000 a year to people who thought he had long since died. And Joseph was sold.

The meeting ended with Joseph agreeing to help, but both men also agreeing not to rush into anything. There was no point in speeding through a program only for it to be destroyed by some problem. Instead, Joseph, Duncan, and others who were rolling up their sleeves for Friends of the Children decided they would launch the program the following academic year, holding regular meetings before then so that everyone could be on the same page.

This gave Duncan and Mike Forzley time to find the right team, starting with their first three Friends. They had identified a couple of key areas of need, including a section of outer Southeast Portland, known appropriately enough as Felony Flats. However, the first three schools they had established a relationship with were—like King Elementary—in Duncan's old neighborhood, North Portland.

It had changed a lot since the old days. Back then, gang-related activity in the blue collar area only ever went as far as a few smashed mailboxes, or the occasional burst of foul language late at night. By the time Friends of the Children was preparing to launch, the area between the neighborhoods of Boise and Eliot was well known throughout the city as a place to avoid.

Duncan, Mike, and Orin were sensitive to the fact that it was a minority neighborhood. They were relying heavily on the power of relationship to transform young lives. They were well aware how potentially offensive it might be for two middle-aged white guys to come in and tell a mostly African-American population of parents that they had the answer to the problems facing their kids. So they were careful to select people from the community who had proven talent for working with kids. The two men were guys who Duncan already knew. Drew was a basketball player, Phil was a musician, and both were well known and respected by local families. Both were African-American, which was a plus; but what they really needed to complete the team was a woman.

They found her when they were least expecting to.

On a school visit one fall morning, they watched as the pupils spilled into the assembly hall. They spotted a short woman, with perfect hair, sitting at the front. Many of the kids ran to her, calling out her name and running up to exchange hugs, to joke and laugh with her.

"Who's that?" Duncan asked the teacher at his side.

"That's Kim. She coaches the girls' drill team. She's a force of nature."

It did not take long to persuade Kim to say yes to the idea of a decent salary in return for spending her week building relationships with a small group of at-risk young people.

Once Kim was locked in, it was time for Friends of the Children to find the first eight children they would work with.

Mike led the initial meetings with teachers across the three target schools. Each one had thrown out the same question: Why limit the number of children to eight per Friend? Some teachers were responsible for whole classrooms full of children who were being raised by grandparents, aunts or foster parents. How could they choose just a handful when all of them were at risk of falling through society's cracks? Each time, Mike took care to explain the reason for the limit. He talked about what they had seen in Baltimore, and shared research that pegged the ideal number of children for a normal mentoring program at around six to ten. Given that the children to whom Kim, Phil, and Drew were going to be devoting themselves would be coming from some extreme backgrounds, and would bring with them all manner of problems, eight was the highest possible number Mike felt comfortable with.

In time, the teachers became the biggest cheerleaders for the project. After all, who among them had entered their profession with no desire to help children? Over the course of a career, too many of them had been witnesses to a slow erosion of that optimistic spirit. Too many of them had lost heart. Friends of the Children vowed to change all that, and if not for a whole class, then at least for a few. It might have been a case of starting small, but the group's ambitions for each child were mighty.

Now it was time to choose.

First, the teachers drew up a shortlist of children they believed were eligible for mentoring. But it wasn't a very short list. Every one of the forty names they put down had a story that sparked compassion. Tales of incarcerated parents and foster care sat alongside childhoods that were at the mercy of grinding poverty and drug addiction. Histories of abuse lined up alongside histories of neglect. All of them had started grade school significantly behind the national average; all faced a seemingly impossible struggle to catch up. None of them had a bright future.

Mike spent weeks observing the children whom teachers had picked out. He sat in on classes, watching as the first graders went about their days largely unaware of the soft-spoken white guy in the corner of the room. He made notes about how they responded to situations in the classroom, and found out about their lives away from school. What was home like? Did they have any means of support? Was there a chance that they had within them the innate seed of resilience that might be enough on its own to see them through? If they did, Mike crossed them off the list.

"This is a reverse draft," Duncan had said so often, and these words looped constantly in Mike's mind as he sat and watched. Friends of the Children didn't want the gifted kids struggling with the fact that their dad was in prison. Friends of the Children didn't want the child whose foster caretaker left them to fend for themselves. They didn't even want the Little Duncans, the ones with street smarts and inner drive. No. Friends of the Children wanted the ones who other charities didn't pick. Friends of the Children wanted the kids whom everyone had given up on: the most challenging children in the whole school.

After all the observations had been carried out, and all the records examined, it was time to meet with the teachers for the selection of the twenty-four children who were going to be the first in the program and assigned to the program's three Friends. It was a brutal meeting; the bright classroom decor and cute classroom displays contrasted starkly with the significance of the event.

Mike led. Five teachers from across three schools were there, as were Joseph and some of the other leaders. Duncan, however, was absent. Even though he had sat in on business meetings where billion-dollar deals were signed, he knew that this was one meeting with which he would not cope well. He knew he would want to rescue every single one.

Everyone watched as Mike wrote up the name of each of the forty children who had been proposed as enrollees into the program. He went down the list one by one, circling those he felt had made it, leaving those who he believed had not. He referred to his notes as he spoke, taking care not to appear formal or flippant. The last thing he wanted to do was to sound like a judge handing down a sentence. Yet, for the teachers of those children who did not make it onto the program, that was exactly what it felt like.

"No!" shouted one teacher as a little girl's name was called out and turned down. "No, Mike. Please don't turn her down. If she doesn't get a Friend, she'll be lost forever."

Other teachers cried, some swore. No one in the room liked seeing those names left alone on the board. It was all too poignant. The enormity of the moment weighed heavily on all of them, as if the air in the classroom had grown thin.

As each name was read out and each child discussed, it grew harder to determine who would get a chance at a better life and who would miss the cut. With every child who did not make it, teachers wondered aloud, "What about the futures of those children?" Surely there couldn't be a second chance at a dramatic intervention such as this?

For all the tension and sorrow that infused the meeting, there was happiness and relief as well among those who made the final decision. It may have been the hardest thing many in the room had ever had to do, but it was also one of the very best.

Once the selections were finalized from King Elementary, Joseph contacted the parents and guardians of those children, a critical moment as the program pushed forward. Knowing that many of them had plenty of encounters with the system—not many of them positive—he knew he had to do all he could to encourage them to believe in the program's potential. He had only been at the school for less than a year, but he was all too familiar with how suspicious many of them felt about big promises. Yet that was precisely what Friends of the Children was offering: a promise so large it would take more than a decade to deliver.

Every one of the eight phone calls Joseph made started the same way. "This is Principal Malone, and I want you to know that I am fully behind what I am about to offer you." He chose his words carefully, telling them that this was a wonderful opportunity. He also worried that if a parent turned down this opportunity for their child because of something he said—or failed to say—the burden would be heavy to bear.

So, much as Duncan had done before him, it fell to Joseph to simply pick up the phone and hope for success. However, unlike the early days of Campbell Global, every one of the phone calls ended in, "Yes."

And so Friends of the Children began.

CHAPTER 8

TILLING THE SOIL

"Breakfast came first, then a teeth cleaning—both of them new experiences for many of the kids."

The wind was cold as Joseph stood in the playground watching a crowd of children swarming Drew. The program had only been running for two months, but the principal had already lost count of the number of times he had heard students ask Drew if he could be their Friend, too. "Don't worry," Joseph said whenever he heard someone ask the question, "I'm here for you. I'll be your ally."

Joseph invested a lot of himself into the early days of Friends of the Children. He got to know all three of the Friends well. He accompanied them on some of their visits with the kids, all the time wanting to get as familiar as possible with the program so that he could help parents understand it. And even though he had to step in on the few occasions in which he thought the Friends were being used as babysitters by parents or guardians, he knew when to stand back and let the relationship develop on its own.

While there were undoubtedly a few teething problems among the parents to deal with, it was the Friends who needed the most guidance—particularly Kim. The problem wasn't anything to do with the way the community responded to her, as once she became a Friend she remained as popular as ever. The problem was that she remained too much a product of her community.

Having grown up in a tough neighborhood, and having failed to graduate high school, Kim had to rely on street smarts to survive. Case in point: when she was shopping one day, she saw one guy hassling another guy. She did what came naturally, reaching into her purse for her gun. Pointing it at the aggressor's nose, she told him to "get the hell out of the store." It was all perfectly understandable, perhaps even excusable, if Kim had visited the store alone. But she had her youth with her.

Orin met with her soon afterward. "Kim," he said, "You can't do that. I know where you live; I get it, but you can't be carrying around a gun in your purse. You're a Friend. You're supposed to be encouraging your girls to find a way out of a life of violence and crime."

She paused and looked at him. "You're full of shit," she said. "You don't know where I live."

The conversation was over.

And with that, Orin set about writing a No Firearms policy for the handbook.

During the first two years there were plenty of other mistakes that led to the learning of valuable lessons. One of them was that Friends should work to encourage other members of the family. Duncan was a season ticketholder with the Portland Trailblazers. He gave seats to any Friend who wanted to take their child to a game. It was a big deal for the kid, who would never have been able to afford to go to an NBA game, let alone get such great seats so close to the action. The Friend would wear a special Friends of the Children jacket, and the Blazers would often acknowledge them over the public address system. What was not to like?

One day, it struck Orin that Friends of the Children's approach to taking kids to the Trailblazers' games wasn't such a wonderful idea after all.

"I'm not happy," he told Duncan, "and I don't like it. We're spoiling these kids. We're missing an important opportunity. They all have under-involved fathers. What if we got the dads to accompany their kids instead of the Friend?"

It was a light bulb moment, and it was later confirmed in a meeting Orin held with Will, a local pastor. Will wasn't a conventional pastor by any means—he had served prison time for murder and now ran a church in his house. But he'd managed to get his life back on track in a way that was evident to all around him. Orin visited the man in his home, intrigued by the way that this muscled, tattooed, and bearded white guy seemed to have such a way of connecting with so many African-American children.

"I hate it when the firemen do their annual Christmas toy drive," Will said as he and Orin sat on his porch. "They say it's for the kids, but then they hand out all the toys themselves. I hate that parents don't get to be involved. So I went to the fire department and told them to change their approach. I suggested they raise the money, get the toys, and bring them to someone like me who could make sure that the parents get them so the parents can give them to their kids. The parents are the ones who can't afford to buy the gifts, but they're the ones who need to be giving them, not you."

Gradually, word leaked out about the test pilot program Friends of the Children had set up with the school that had managed to start working in the toughest, least accessible area of the city. People started to take notice, which was useful because the project needed money. Duncan's gift had guaranteed that the initial twenty-four children would all have Friends—salaried and trained mentors—to work with them all the way through high school, but everyone involved in Friends of the Children knew that there were a lot more than twenty-four children who needed help. If the project was to make any kind of impact in its chosen neighborhoods, let alone in the Portland metro area, they would need to find a lot more money. And while Duncan was rich, he wasn't that rich. Besides, he had no desire to be the sole source of funding. He wanted others to be able to share the joy of giving to this work, the kind that promised to transform lives. More importantly, Duncan wanted Friends of the Children to take root in the local community so that the citywide community would catch the vision and take ownership of the program.

Orin knew the way the system worked, having already made dozens of successful grant applications while at the Morrison Center. Since their project was still small, it could only really hope to secure funding from local trusts and charitable foundations. To be able to make a case to the national players, such as the Ford Foundation—and access the kind of support they offered—Friends of the Children would have to show that they had some serious backers behind them. They needed a small trust with a strong enough reputation to impress these national players.

Orin and Duncan discussed it. "No problem," he said. "I've got a good track record with just the right kind of trust. I can submit a strong proposal to them." Orin didn't just write a strong proposal; he was convinced when he'd finished that it was the best he'd ever created. He sent a draft of it to a friend of his, who happened to be the director of the trust, receiving a glowing report from him.

The trouble was, the rest of the board didn't see it that way. They voted the application down, six to one.

"I'm sorry," his friend said when he phoned with the news. "The board just couldn't get past the fact that you want to spend all this money on just eight kids. And even if they did make the grant, they don't see how anyone else will ever step in to make the next round of funding. It's all just so…" he paused, searching for the right word.

"Contrarian?" suggested Orin.

"Yes. What you're doing is too far out there, Orin. I'm sorry."

Orin was aware of the fact that his friend hated it when people went behind his back, but what other choice did he have now? He called up another board member right away. "Warren," he said, "you're making a big mistake. Come with me at 9 a.m. on Thursday, and I'll show you why."

Warren did what he was told.

Orin introduced him to Phil, Drew, and Kim—who, thankfully, was on her best behavior—and with a number of children who were not.

But as a result of this meeting, the next time the board met, they voted six to one in favor of the grant.

And as a result of that, Friends of the Children closed out its first year having secured $250,000 in funding over the following three years.

In year two, they took on another three Friends and an additional twenty-four children. They also teamed up with AmeriCorps, then in its infancy, which provided twenty volunteers—taking on four kids each. In one year, Friends of the Children had grown from working with twenty-four kids to 128 kids. And still, the organization was barely touching the surface of the problem.

Working with AmeriCorps wasn't all smooth sailing. The volunteers were supposed to be with Friends for just one year, maybe two at most. The resultant potential disruption to the kids especially bothered Duncan in particular. When nine of the eleven volunteers left at the end of their first year, it confirmed his worst fears; and at the end of its second year, Friends withdrew from its partnership with AmeriCorps. All eighty children who had been mentored by them were taken on by new full time, fully employed Friends—and that included some who wished to remain. It was disruptive for the kids, but it ultimately played an important role in defining Friends of the Children as a professional organization committed to working with children over the long haul.

Not everything about AmeriCorps was awkward, however. There was an increase in staff, even after the dissolution of the partnership, which allowed Friends to work in five new schools. Some were in Southeast Portland in Felony Flats, which was highly different from North Portland. It was largely white, for one; and while the first Friends did encounter violence and gang activity in Portland's other neighborhoods, those working with children in Felony Flats faced a darker side of poverty, the cyclical kind, which weighs down families for generation after generation.

Sarah, one of the AmeriCorps volunteers who would go on to become a fully employed Friend and staff member for decades to come, spotted the dangers facing her children as their first year of working together drew to a close. School played an important role for the kids, and the idea of three months of summer vacation spent outside the stability inherent in the normal school routine left Sarah—and others—worried. Would the kids get enough food during the day? How much further would they fall behind academically before school started up again? What might be the effects of three months of exposure, twenty-four hours a day, seven days a week, to continual neglect or worse?

Friends of the Children decided to host a daily summer school. Each day started with them driving out to collect their kids as they passed the summer between second and third grade. Few of the homes they visited ever had a locking front door. Most of the time the Friends would just let themselves in, bracing for the worst.

Inside these homes, they found little ones like Nate, who was always wearing the same filthy clothes, always sitting on the floor, on his own in a house where his dad barely seemed to notice him. They found kids like Mikey, a child whose anger was always just a hair's breadth away from full on meltdown. Like most of the others, Mikey never had his own bed, or even his own shoes. Often the Friend found children they'd never seen before, sleeping on the kitchen or bathroom floor, like tired ghosts.

Then there were kids like Falisha. She always needed careful handling, too, but in a different way. Her mom was developmentally disabled, and her dad lived in the basement. Day or night, any visitor could hear him shouting profanities and cussing out his kids from his underground cave. The few occasions on which he did emerge, Sarah knew that his violent temper could take over at any time. Throughout the house the floors were always covered with human excrement, urine, and vomit, all giving off their own unique fumes as the house baked beneath the summer sun. Sarah learned the hard way how to suppress her gag reflex, to be cordial, and get out quickly.

Back at the park—where the Friends had set up summer school in a building whose purpose had long been forgotten—they set to work. Breakfast came first, then teeth cleaning. Both were new experiences for many of the kids. After that they helped the kids with their reading and writing, perhaps a little math as well. None of it was too intense, and the main aim was always that the kids would leave feeling nurtured and cared for.

Over the summer, the Friends saw progress. Nate, who had always been easygoing and happy-go-lucky, soaked up every ounce of the positive attention he received. Mikey became more trusting as he realized that the Friends weren't going anywhere.

Falisha, whom Sarah had never heard utter a kind word about herself, finally had a breakthrough one morning. She handed Sarah a piece of writing she had just completed.

"This is really good work," Sarah said, once she had finished reading.

Falisha, as ever, stared back, her face locked, betraying no emotion at all. But then, for the first time in the whole summer, she smiled.

CHAPTER 9

MORE THAN A FRIEND

"They were children. Nothing less. And the Friends were not social workers, substitute teachers or baby sitters; they were friends. Nothing less."

Ava was six years old when she was asked whether she would like Sarah to be her Friend. She just shrugged. At that point in her life, a lot of people had come and gone. Her parents had separated and both had already spent more time in jail than they had with her and her two brothers. When her mom and dad were both locked up, Ava either went to live with her grandma or another family member whom Department of Human Services found. When one of her parents was released, the parent would gather up the children and move to some new corner of the city. But while the streets were unfamiliar to Ava, the sights and sounds always remained the same: her mom passed out on a couch surrounded by charred glass tubes and discarded lighters, her dad shouting on the street before storming inside and tearing the house apart, eyes as black as bowling balls. Sometimes, when

Ava was out on the streets following her big brother around, she forgot where she lived. And sometimes, when she couldn't remember, she wished she could.

When Ava joined the program, she met with Sarah every week. It took months of hanging out, braiding hair, visiting the park, and looking at books in the library before enough trust was formed, and Ava began to speak about what life was really like for her. Gradually she started to share the stories of what happened at home with Sarah.

It was only when they had been together for two years that Ava trusted Sarah enough to share one of her most treasured secrets. "I know what I want to be when I grow up," Ava said as they sat in Sarah's car one day after school.

Sarah listened, wondering what career choice the eight-year-old girl would go for. A nurse or teacher was plausible, but pop star or actress seemed like a stronger bet.

"I want to be in *Playboy*," Ava said.

Life descended deeper into chaos as Ava and her siblings were moved from place to place according to their parents' whims. By the time she was in fifth grade, Ava had attended four different schools. There were times when Sarah would arrive at the address at which she had seen Ava the week before, finding no one there. Neighbors were never able to offer much help, and all Sarah could do was call Ava's grandmother and ask if she knew where Ava was. Most of the time, Ava's grandmother helped, but there was always a tone of weary heaviness to her voice.

About the only familiar thing for Ava was the way her parents behaved. At any given point her mom was either her best friend or her worst enemy, and there were times when, from the minute she sat down in Sarah's car to the minute she said goodbye, Ava vented about how much she hated the woman.

Her father's drug addiction kept him on a tight leash. After a particularly long jail stint, he got out and moved in with a woman who was equally addicted to drugs and self-destruction. The two of them dragged each other down into a world of heroin and crystal meth, welcoming the oblivion, embracing the numbness. Miraculously, he woke up to the fact that he was on the verge of losing his children permanently. The fear was strong enough to break through his addiction, and he checked into rehab. He got a job in a school cafeteria, and took Ava and one of her brothers back into custody.

For nine glorious months, all was well. "He's finally a dad," Ava told Sarah, a smile covering her face wider than ever before.

It didn't last. Her dad disappeared before he'd been sober for a year, and Ava retreated to the safety of her isolation. She still participated in the overnight camps and the swimming trips she had always enjoyed with Sarah, but there was hesitation in her. Again Sarah worried about what kind of future she was facing. What outcome would be successful? At times, Sarah thought if she could just prevent Ava from becoming a prostitute, she would have achieved something remarkable.

But Campbells don't quit, and neither do Friends.

As Ava entered her teenage years, Sarah carried on as she

had before; tracking her down when she moved to a new home, picking her up after school, listening to her talk about the new friends she was making. Sarah tried desperately not to appear judgmental whenever Ava talked about how much she liked certain guys, even though they all carried weapons and did a lot of fighting.

Sarah's car became their sanctuary. In the trunk she kept a storage box, in which she kept the souvenirs Ava always gave her whenever she left one house and moved on to another. Other things went into the box as well: special work from school that Ava pretended not to care about, ticket stubs from days out together, photos of the two of them goofing off. And when, twelve years after they'd first met, Ava graduated high school—on time—Sarah presented her with a book that contained all the treasures the box had guarded for so long.

Perhaps the best sign of all that Friends of the Children had served Ava well came a couple of years later. Like every child in the program, Ava aged out of it when she graduated high school, but her friendship with Sarah continued. "I'm pregnant," Ava said one day. She was twenty. The only positive parenting she had experienced in her life was a short time for a few months in which her dad was sober. Sarah was nervous about her pregnancy. And yet somehow, Ava made it through pregnancy and into parenthood with grace and flair. As much as her parents ignored their children, Ava devoted herself to hers. Against all the odds, she made it out of her own childhood okay.

Friends of the Children learned to evolve and grow with

every year that passed, with every child who graduated. They learned through relationships like Sarah and Ava's that a Friend would often become a part of the family. So Friends of the Children enacted a policy that banned any Friend from ever taking a briefcase or a clipboard anywhere near any of their children. And no kid would ever be referred to as "a client" or "a case." They were children. Nothing less. And the Friends were not social workers, substitute teachers, or baby sitters; they were *friends*. Nothing less.

Of the first three Friends, Drew and Kim were the ones who stayed the longest. However, Phil moved on quickly, allowing Friends of the Children to further clarify their thinking on what a good Friend should be. And while their initial instincts had led them to believe that Friends should come from the same community as the children they worked with, experience taught them that other factors were more important. While it was good to know the streets the kids came from, if the Friend had no knowledge of life beyond the community, it would be almost impossible to introduce them to a wider world with fresh possibilities. From that point forward, Friends were also required to have college degrees.

There were other discussions as well, like whether the Friends should just focus exclusively on their children or whether they could—or should—expand their work to offer support to parents and siblings.

As ever, the conversation started when a Friend told the rest of the team about a kid he had met.

Matt had joined as a Friend when the first large grant funding had come through. He was in his mid twenties, tall, and practical as he was down to earth. He was never seen without his battered Stanford cap, and liked to wear socks with his sandals.

He had been paired with Logan, a boy suffering from developmental difficulties. The story was that his mother's longstanding drug addiction had reached a peak when she was pregnant with him, leaving Logan with a severe speech impediment and plenty of behavioral issues. Matt liked the boy immediately, and started by taking him for ice cream and visiting the park that lay across the road from the house where he lived.

A few weeks in, Matt visited the Friends of the Children office, looking for help.

"It's this kid, Logan," he told the program manager. "He's not the only one in the family who needs help. There are two sisters and a brother, a grandmother, and a great-grandmother trying to bring them up. The mom's addicted to crack, and there's Aunt Amy who shows up from time to time, terrifying the crap out of all of them. The old ladies are trying their best, but it's toxic around there. At best, they're just surviving. The oldest girl is retreating from the world. They're all vulnerable, but if we could just get a Friend for that one girl…"

It sounded as though Matt might be right, but the program was full already. By now, the policy had shifted so that Friends started work with kindergarten kids, not first graders. There was no way a second-grade girl and a third-grade boy could be brought on board so late. All the research suggested that the earlier mentoring started, the better.

"Okay," said Matt. "But can someone at least help out

with the oldest girl's hair? It can't have been brushed in years. It's matted like you wouldn't believe."

Matt's manager relented. It wasn't such a bad thing for a Friend to be so driven by compassion.

A few days later Matt showed up at the office with Logan and his two eldest siblings. "This is Samuel," he said, introducing the older boy, who forced a smile. "And this is Nicky. She lives over by the park with the tall cedar trees."

So far, life had taught Nicky to be wary of everyone. Her aunt's cruelty, and her mother's absence, had reinforced the conclusion that she would only cope in life if she remained quiet and out of the way of others. Meeting and getting to know Matt had been hard enough, but being introduced to others like this was difficult for Nicky. She appeared to be nothing short of terrified. She hung her head and tried to hide behind her shoulders, like a bird whose wings had been torn from its back.

The manager—Deb—and another Friend, convinced Nicky to sit down and trust them enough to start working on her hair. It was matted as though it had been baked in molasses; lice were thriving within its dark recesses. Dealing with lice was nothing new to Deb and the Friend, but Nicky had it worse than the others they'd seen. They made slow progress. After two hours, the worst of the knots were out. More importantly, Nicky had finally relaxed enough to eat some of the candy that Deb had been offering her throughout.

Matt brought Nicky back every week, Deb each time making further progress with her hair, Nicky each time inching toward being able to trust them.

Nicky had been interested in Friends of the Children ever since little Logan had come home and told her that some weird guy in a red cap had been looking at him from the back of the classroom all week. When she finally met Matt—red cap in place just as described, toes pushing his socks out through the ends of his sandals—she agreed with her little brother's assessment: definitely weird.

Nicky did what she always did. She kept quiet, observing. She was shy and timid and she didn't like talking to new people or to strangers. In part, she later admitted that her withdrawal was driven by fear, but that was not the whole story. Retreating and watching what people did allowed her to judge whether a person could be trusted or not. With a mom whose moods changed dependent upon what drugs she took, and an aunt who thrived on spewing harsh words in an instant, Nicky had already figured out what she needed to do to survive. And it depended upon her ability to be able to watch people and read what was going on beneath the surface.

It did not take long for her to trust Matt. He showed up to take Logan out to the park, suggesting that the other kids come, too. He bought the ice cream, which Nicky and Samuel ate as they sat on one of the lower limbs of the cedar trees. She observed everything that went on below her, and she evidently liked what she saw.

Then, an extra space opened up in the program. A girl moved away, leaving a Friend with an opening for a child. Deb had been stirred by the stories of what home life was like for

Nicky, and even though the girl was already in third grade, she bent the rules just enough to make sure that it was Nicky who got the slot.

By now, Friends of the Children had developed solid policies for how long a Friend would stay with a child. While Sarah kept the same eight kids throughout the twelve years they were in the program, new children who got invited on were told they could expect to have two or three Friends over the years. And so it was for Nicky. Her first Friend built on the foundation of trust Matt had established, while her second encouraged Nicky to be bolder. Together they took trips to Taco Bell, where Nicky had to order her own food. The first time it took her thirty minutes to summon the courage, but in time the words, "A bean burrito and a Pepsi, please," came more readily when she needed them.

These basic life skills—talking to strangers, deciding on and then ordering what she wanted, asking for help when she needed it—were the kind of thing that almost every Friend invested in with kids like Nicky. And learning to explore the world outside the neighborhood was an equally vital step. Even if they started with something as uneventful as a bean burrito and a soda, these trips made a lasting impression.

Friends always spent plenty of time in school, checking in with teachers, providing extra support if necessary. Their mere presence at school also sent an unspoken message that the halls of education were where foundations for a better future were laid. Nicky's mom had dropped out of school in seventh grade, while her aunt and grandma had managed to graduate from high school, but barely. Nicky had lost count of the number of times her aunt had told her she would never become anything more than a drug addict like her mom. While the words indeed wounded her at first, as she settled in at school and chose to dedicate herself to her studies, she decided to prove her aunt wrong.

Like Duncan.

It drove the woman insane.

In fifth grade, Nicky came home from school one day to find Matt and her Friend, Diana, already there, waiting for Logan and the others.

"Your great grandmother's sick; she's at the hospital," Matt said. Nicky later admitted that she would've been desperately worried, too, but something about the way he reassured them gave her peace about the situation. Matt told them that she had pneumonia and would need to be taken care of for a few days. He got them to pack and took them to the house that Duncan had bought years before—the Friends' House, the place where kids and their Friends hung out, did homework, and learned basic homemaking skills, such as laundry, cooking, and cleaning.

"We're all going to stay at the Friends' House until she gets out, okay?" he said.

It was a simple gesture, but it had a major impact on Nicky. At the end of the three-night stay, when her great grandma got out of the hospital and the kids went back home, Nicky was left with a new appreciation of how much Matt and Diana cared.

Nicky struggled, however, when Diana left to go on maternity leave. Now in the seventh grade, she was devastated by the sudden onrush of an old and familiar fear of abandonment. But in Diana's place came Luci. As Nicky quickly grew to trust her, she realized how far she had come. The shy girl was long gone; the fear of abandonment quickly passed.

Nicky became an avid reader and sportswoman. The more time she spent around her Friend, the more she started to think about college. She knew she wanted to be like her older brother, Samuel, and attend college somewhere, but she had no idea where to go or what to study. She and Luci talked about it a lot, having conversations that no adult at home would be able to share with Nicky. Luci described what college life had been like in her own experience.

"And remember," she told Nicky, "it's possible for you to do anything."

Nicky liked that idea. But how would she ever pay for it?

In the winter during ninth grade, all thoughts of college were swept away when her grandmother passed away. Her life changed in a moment. Her mom was still on drugs; she was in no state to be able to step in as the primary caregiver for the three children who were still living with her at home. Samuel was away at college, and though he offered to quit and return, nobody would let him. That opened the door for the worst of all options: Nicky's aunt flew back from Texas with her new husband.

"You're going to have to come and live with me," she told them, pretty much right after she walked into the house.

Nicky thought about what life would be like with her aunt. She pictured a small town, population 1,000 people, with one stoplight. She imagined the effort it would take for her to resist her aunt's constant attacks. She pictured herself climbing trees again. She wondered if there would be any that were tall enough.

"No," Nicky said. She was standing up to her Aunt Amy for the first time in her life. "We're not moving."

Aunt Amy's face soured even more. "We'll talk about this after the funeral."

The funeral took place in typical Portland weather, beneath gray skies leaking raindrops throughout the day. As the service ended, and the family and the guests drove back to the house, Matt turned to Nicky and her three siblings—Samuel, Logan, and Sheila—in the car.

"I'm leaving my position at Friends of the Children," he said. "I'm moving in with you. I'll make sure your rent gets paid, and that you have food and clothes. I'll be there until Sheila graduates."

No one from Friends of the Children had ever done anything like this. It was unorthodox, perhaps a little unwise and maybe even risky, but Matt had already discussed it with Duncan and Deb.

"I can't let their aunt take them," he'd told them, "and if they slip into the foster system there's no way all three kids will be kept together. I can't let that happen. I just can't."

There wasn't much more to be said.

CHAPTER 10

A RUDDER FOR LIFE

"Surely he was going to follow in
his older brother's footsteps and join a gang."

I t would require a long list to be able to catalogue each and every one of Duncan Campbell's idiosyncrasies. After a lifetime of hard work, high risk, and proven success, he had entered the last third of his life with a freedom to work in a manner that could produce the best results. Therefore, regardless of what was going on around him, at any point Duncan would break away from the action and frantically scribble on a Post-it® note, scraps of paper, napkin, or whatever else comes to hand. To the observer, the scratched lines and random words made little sense, but to Duncan these transcriptions of his real-time thinking were an essential tool that allowed him to develop new ideas, and work through troublesome problems. Every good idea or musing that he had was captured in this way. Nothing was allowed to fade away.

These notes—often no bigger than the palm of his hand—were then collated into groups, stapled onto a sheet of paper, and placed into one of the many folders he kept close by in his mobile filing cabinet—which, only occasionally—happened to double as the back seat of his car. In time, each and every one of those folders was taken to one of the many storage units Duncan kept around Portland. Inside those windowless rooms, into cardboard boxes labeled and organized by year, Duncan carefully placed every folder. No thought, no idea, no hunch or musing that he'd ever had disappeared. It was a library of everything of note that his brain had ever focused on. It was a living library of ideas, a paper trail of thought.

And then there was the dancing. Duncan loved to dance. He'd make sure he was in town every time a big name artist— or an underground indie sensation—played in Portland. Whether it was a stadium-sized anthem from a rock legend or a deep techno soundtrack in a late night club, Duncan was there, bouncing, smiling, outlasting pretty much everyone else. His reputation as a mover and a shaker spread so far that one year Friends of the Children put on a whole fundraising event called Dancing with Duncan. Most of the guys were wallflowers nursing their drinks, but Duncan, silver-haired and eyes on full sparkle, traced graceful patterns on the floor, taking each partner for a spin like a matinee idol from a bygone era.

Duncan was a profligate fist bumper, and no encounter with a Friend or child would be allowed to begin or end without knuckle touching knuckle. Even the regular board meetings started this way, as one or two Friends came in and told those gathered about some of the children they were working with. The glimpses of hope or despair they revealed played an important part in keeping the organization firmly rooted and focused.

There were so many more of these memorable moments with Duncan, but none were as engaging or captivating as the way he responded to the very children he set out to help. Nothing compared to the palpable thrill he got when he met up with a former child of the program. They were, after all, the reason why he did what he did.

"I'm so proud of you, Robert," Duncan said as he sat grinning opposite an equally excited looking senior at the University of Oregon. Robert is vice president of the university's student body, and plans to go to law school. "What you did, and what you're going to do, it's…" He paused. "It's remarkable."

Robert's story was vintage Friends of the Children. Like many who had been helped by the program, he faced the unholy trinity of life experience that so often led to gang involvement: he was African-American, had a crack addict mom and an absent father, and lived in a section of the city controlled by gangs. Surely he was destined to follow in his older brother's footsteps and join a gang.

Along with his older brother and sister, Robert grew up moving from home to home. The kids rarely lived with their mother, who would take off without warning for long periods of time. Sometimes she left them with her best friend, who was equally ill-equipped to care for children. Other times she just told the boys to do whatever their sister told them. They were the kinds of kids who grow up to become statistics, the ones who go bad and leave people wondering how it all went wrong.

How did it go wrong? The answer was simple: they didn't have any positive influences in their lives.

So Robert had to grow up fast. Even at a young age, when his birthdays could still be counted on the fingers of one hand, he had to learn how to spot danger on the street. When a pit bull attacked him as he walked home from the park with his little sister, there was no one else around to step in. Robert alone had to get himself and his sister to safety. Or when he found a lighter under his bed and decided to see what would happen when he used it to set fire to the bedding. He quickly—and painfully—learned what it felt like for his mom to be so mad at him that he had to spend a week living with a friend until she cooled down. Or the time at King Elementary when he was going outside to the porta potty with his best friend, Kyle—the one with the cornrows of which Robert had always been jealous. Midway through relieving himself, Robert looked down to see Kyle worming his head directly into the porta potty. Though he tried to avoid it, Robert urinated on his best friend's head. That was the day he learned what it felt like to get the biggest ass-whooping ever from his mom and become one of the few kids ever to get suspended from kindergarten.

He learned other lessons that year. Tougher ones. He discovered what life was like for a child whose mother leaves and never comes back. He was too young to really understand that her drug addiction was at the root of her exit from family life. All he really knew at the time was that she said she was going to California and she never came back.

Robert's dad had never really been much for commitment, and eventually the state realized the extent of the situation and stepped in. That meant that Robert and his siblings were paraded before social workers and foster care workers as yet another set of children on the verge of being sucked into the system. Social workers began the protocol to take custody of the children. However, Robert's aunt Mary, a woman who lived a life so completely different from her sister's, decided she would take care of them.

Mary saw the direction Robert was headed, and she knew the typical outcome. From her experience working as a corrections officer, she knew that a child needed someone to emulate, a guide he or she could imitate as the child discovered the value and importance of morals and values. If children don't get that by the time they reach twelve, it can all be too late.

She found it hard to fathom how Robert could avoid the same kind of fate as the people she worked with. Over the years, she got to know some of the repeat offenders, and asked them where and how they thought things had started to fall apart for them. Drugs, single parents, getting in trouble at an early age, no one to help them turn things around: their lists sounded similar to Robert's plight.

So, despite the fact that Mary was nursing her own husband as he battled cancer, she invited Robert and his siblings in. When Robert, his sister, and his brother moved in, the total number of children in the household rose to nine.

Always a smart kid, Robert was nevertheless late to learn

how and when to put a leash on his tongue. So when he
picked up that the reason for his uncle's absence from the
house was that he was sick, he didn't hesitate to inform his
cousin.

"Your dad's dying of cancer," he said shortly before
getting another whipping to rival even the punishment
handed out after the incident with the kid with the cornrows
and the porta potty.

Eventually his uncle died, leaving Aunt Mary to bring up
all nine children on what little money she earned as a
corrections officer, even with overtime. She made sure that
the kids were fed and that they got to school on time. Robert
saw himself as an outsider, though, abandoned by his mom,
an inconvenience to his aunt. And when his older brother left
and moved into a foster home, Robert and his sister felt
unwelcome.

"Jo-Jo's gone and Mom's not coming back," his sister said
one day. "We're going to have to grow up."

Even with the best of intentions, Mary could see Robert
was slipping through the cracks. She had too many children
to care for, too little time to earn too little money. She simply
didn't have time or enough resources to give him what he
needed.

When Mary first heard about Friends of the Children, she
was hesitant. Her work in corrections made her wonder what
kind of adult would want to spend time with underprivileged
children. She looked for red flags, suspicious that these
so-called "Friends" were really just attracted to children in an
unhealthy way, using the organization as cover to meet them.

She started to ask around. Mary sought out information about the program, the leaders, and the people who worked there. When she saw that they were there for the long haul, she changed her initial assessment, wondering whether she might just have found the program that could help slam on the brakes for Robert.

She was right. Javier became the Friend Robert never knew he needed. Javier was the support Mary learned to rely on. When a teacher was having problems with Robert, it was his Friend, Javier, who met with the teacher. He observed the way Robert sensed weakness in people, the way he would push their buttons to make them angry, then back away, claiming he was the victim. Javier saw the way Robert caused havoc and wore his teachers down.

He made sure Robert was focusing on his studies. He talked to him about how other people perceived him, and listened when Robert explained that he hated the way people talked about him.

"What do they say?" Javier asked.

"They say, 'Robert, you little bastard.'"

And as he listened, Javier heard the truth: Robert was lonely, he was scared. He always felt like he was an outsider.

While outside observers will never see a Friend carrying a briefcase or a clipboard, it doesn't mean that the time they spend with their children is a succession of random and unplanned moments. Every Friend creates a plan for the areas they want to work on with their children, and every activity is approached with a view to moving their child a little closer toward their goal.

For Javier, it was clear what Robert needed. His own parents were barely teenagers when he was born. Javier instantly recognized Robert's need for guidance and support. Through a turbulent and precarious childhood, Robert needed something—or someone—who was solid. He needed someone who would be consistent, who would educate him in all the little life lessons that a parent should deliver as a matter of course.

Some of these lessons were constructed around the way Robert interacted with people when he was in public. There was no doubt that Robert's veneer of self-confidence was engaging and funny, and Javier had seen it in action from the very start.

Robert had barreled up to him and told him, "I'm really fast," before running off around the kindergarten playground like a pinball.

"Yes," Javier said, "for a little fat kid you do move pretty quick."

At other times—like when talking with his cousin about cancer—Robert's mouth could get him into trouble. When Robert was a teenager, Javier took him to a college basketball game. Robert was a big Oregon State fan at the time, and he spent the entire game talking about how much he disliked one of the teams on the court—the University of Oregon. At some point early on he noticed that a couple of his digs at the University of Oregon had raised a smile or two from the spectators around them, and he upped his volume and increased the pace of his delivery as the game went on. In time, people were laughing, but in an awkward, uncomfortable way. He was on a roll, oblivious to the mild offense he was causing the visiting fans as he ripped into their alma mater.

"Did you notice how people reacted to you?" Javier asked as they shuffled out of the bleachers at the end.

"No," said Robert. "Wait, yes—they were laughing at me, right? They thought I was funny."

"No," said Javier. "That was not what they were thinking."

Robert still had much to learn.

Friends of the Children provided Robert with an education that went far beyond the lessons he was sitting through in his crowded, raucous school rooms filled with students almost as rambunctious as Robert.

Not every child connects with his or her Friend, and it requires a certain degree of synergy to happen for the relationship to thrive. Javier instinctively knew that if Robert really engaged with the mentoring process, there would be no stopping him. All that untapped teenage potential could be unleashed, flowing out into what was sure to be a remarkable life.

But he also knew what it would look like if the relationship failed to thrive.

After Robert and his siblings transitioned from their aunt Mary's house, they found a new home in foster care. Robert's brother, Joe, settled into life in the foster home. It was a poor environment to grow up in; a house full of boys whose parents were either dead, missing or incarcerated and a foster care worker whose motivation to open up his home only went as far as the paycheck. There were wild days and even wilder nights—and soon the pack of boys formed their own gang. Though he also had a Friend and was in the program, the odds were stacked so heavily against Joe that he soon chose to live his life the way it was lived on the streets. Petty crime flowed into more serious affairs, and soon he began the shuffle between time in prison and temporary bursts of freedom.

Yet Robert watched his brother's path, opening his eyes to the future ahead of him if he followed him down such a path. Instead of following his brother, Robert embraced what Javier was offering him with a passion. He trusted his Friend, and was happy to follow him wherever he led. Even all the way to Seattle.

As an adolescent, the Seattle to Portland (STP) bike ride was the perfect opportunity for Robert to learn how to channel his inner resilience. It was a grueling challenge, 200 miles of riding over one or two days, with almost 6,000 feet of climbing beneath the mid-July sun. For a twelve-year-old kid with excess weight and minimal experience in strenuous physical challenges, the training alone was a daunting task. But Javier believed in him. That was enough to get them started.

Their training plan was simple enough; they cycled up hills. Lots of hills. And if ever Robert decided to get off and walk up, Javier would gently but firmly encourage him to coast back down the bottom and start again. Once he'd conquered the hill, they'd move on to another one, and another, each one taller than the last. When, eventually, Robert groaned his way up to the top of a peak so high that every one of the five miles on the way up had felt like a lifetime of pain, Javier was right next to him. "Good job," he said, quietly. "If you can do this hill, there's nothing you can't do."

Robert needed constant reminding. Battling against a vicious headwind in 100-degree heat one day, Robert fell behind. Eventually, tears streaking down his face, he caught up with Javier. "I quit!" he said. "I can't go any farther."

"But," Javier said, "we're almost there. Once we get there we can turn around, then we'll have a tailwind behind us."

Robert slumped over his handlebars, the tears still falling. "But my water bottle fell off."

"Okay, well, you keep going. I'll catch up."

They managed it, although there were more tears and more stops. And the next morning, when Javier knocked on Robert's door and told him it was time to get back out on the road and continue with their training, Robert didn't protest. He knew he could trust his Friend. Lots of times they would get a ride out to a point thirty miles from the finish line and bike the route back in to Portland.

It wasn't until the final morning of the race itself that Robert finally understood why his training had been so difficult. It was early on a Sunday morning. The sun was rising and the air was beginning to lose the chill of darkness. Every bit of Robert was aching from the 170 miles he had cycled already. During the weeks of training he had never felt quite as tired as he did at that point, and he had been pushed so many times when he had felt far lighter twinges of pain. But not this time. This was a race he was going to finish, no matter what. As he paused at the rest stop, he looked around. It was the very place where he and Javier had started so many of their training rides. It was familiar; it was known.

"I know where we are," he said. "We're going to make it."

There was one last mile-long hill waiting for them as they closed in on the finish line. "You're tired, and this is going to be tough," said Javier. But he didn't need to speak. Robert's head was down, his legs slowly turning the pedals, his breathing heavy but steady. They were some of the last few out on the course, but Robert would receive no assistance. He pushed and pushed, digging deep into his reserves of confidence and strength. He pushed through the doubt, the pain, and the fear that he might not make it after all. He pushed until the finish came into view and he and Javier had to navigate their way around the workers who were busy dismantling the crowd barriers. He pushed until he crossed the finish line, savoring the sense of satisfaction and pride. These would never leave him.

It's easy to give kids like Robert cheap awards to try to boost their self esteem, and there's a place for trophies and competition that come without a grueling price tag of personal sacrifice and relentless commitment. But those rewards are thin and evaporate too easily. For Robert, the Seattle to Portland ride was everything it could have been. It showed him just what he was capable of achieving as well as what he was capable of enduring. It showed him how it was possible to rely on a relationship, how a Friend could be with you all the way through a seemingly impossible challenge. And it showed him that despite what was happening to his brother Joe and despite what had happened to his mom, he had the power to choose to push through. After years of wanting to tell people that he was fast or show them that he was funny, he could finally know for himself something that was perfectly honest and indisputably true about him; that he was not a quitter.

Robert is a classic example of a child in the program. As he made his way through high school, there were the inevitable mistakes and mess ups, the crises caused by too many tensions at home and too much pressure elsewhere, but Robert was always willing to pause, to call up Javier and seek his advice. And when that advice was hard to hear, requiring him to eat some humble pie and apologize to his aunt or let go of being right, he remembered what it felt like to have his body pressed down onto the bike, forcing his way up hill after hill, never giving up, never getting off.

***

SITTING OPPOSITE ROBERT, DUNCAN couldn't stop smiling. "It's been four years since you graduated the program, and look at you now. You're a senior in college, you're going to study law, and you're vice president of the student body. You're already a leader. Just think what the rest of your life holds for you."

The feeling of respect and admiration was mutual. "People say I've had a crazy life," said Robert. "But I say, 'What part was crazy?' To me it was normal because I lived it. And I knew that one day each week I would be okay because I could see Javier."

There are a lot of things that a Friend is not; not a social worker, not a teacher, not a parent. They are just a *friend*. But that word "just" doesn't belong in that sentence. There is nothing small or insignificant about friendship. In a life scarred by neglect, cracked through by missed opportunity and exposed to all kinds of risk by poverty, a Friend has the potential to completely transform a life.

"That bike ride taught me so much," said Robert. "I have so many trophies from sports, but that's the one I value the most. That's the one that taught me how a man is supposed to act in the face of adversity. I wouldn't have it if not for Javier and for the program. Friends of the Children gave me a Friend and a father figure when I had none. You gave me a rudder."

"A rudder?" said Duncan.

He nodded. "One time we were on a camp out. Javier said to me that everyone has a rudder on their heart, and that different things we hear or experience change the direction of the rudder. Javier was my rudder. He was the fixture in my life that showed me where to go. He changed my perception of who I am and who I had to be. He's been the only person I could ever count on."

CHAPTER 11

LITTLE NINJA, LITTLE STEPS

"He merely stepped back and let Troy wander in."

From the very beginning, Orin and Duncan wanted a study performed on their practices. Orin's background in clinical practice had taught him that if Friends of the Children was going to be as effective as everyone believed it could be, they would need more than emotive stories and anecdotal evidence. In order to ramp up the program and make a powerful difference on the numbers of at-risk children in America, they needed to win over policy makers and the biggest potential supporters. To do that they would simply have to have compelling, rigorous, and verifiable evidence that what they were doing worked.

One of Duncan's concerns was a practical matter. His years in Campbell Global taught him that, of all the ingredients of success, focus was the most essential. If Friends of the Children diverted their attention and resources away from direct work with the kids, even if it was for the fuller study of program methods and results, Duncan feared that the work itself would suffer, especially in the early years.

Yet that wasn't the whole story. They were proposing a longitudinal study, the kind in which children who had been accepted into the program would be tracked throughout their twelve years alongside a randomly assigned control group of children who were similarly at risk when in kindergarten but who were not being helped in any way by Friends of the Children.

There were good reasons why he had never sat in on a selection meeting, why he had never accompanied his staff as they visited yet another school to view potential kids that might—or might not—be invited the join the program. For Duncan, the idea of turning away children who needed help was a moral dilemma. Those children who would form the control group—children who needed a Friend just as badly as those who had been accepted into the program—would be like lab rats. There was no way that Duncan could agree to this at this early stage of the program. "Not yet, at least," he said, when Orin first brought it up in the early days. "Let's hone the model first."

It was hard to define what honing actually looked like. After all, progress can be unlocked in so many ways. For Robert it was a bicycle, while Nicky's early victories came in the form of a successful order of bean burritos without feeling paralyzed by fear and shyness. For a kid called Little Ninja, it all started with an alarm clock.

The trip to Little Ninja's home was Troy's first home visit. As a new Friend he had been given a little background and told what to expect, but the experience still shocked him. As soon as he pulled up outside he could see several cars littering the yard like whales beached in a storm. He saw fish tanks lying among them like fallen tombstones, some empty, others full of algae, none of them in any state to support life. Toys were scattered across the yard, and every window he could see from the street appeared to be lined with dark material. It was late afternoon in summer and the house looked as though it had been abandoned for years.

All of this was exactly what Troy had been told to expect. The two pit bulls roaming between the chain link fence and the house were something else. He was not comfortable around dogs at the best of times, let alone when standing on a street in Felony Flats where he had been told to avoid as a young child. Looking over his shoulder, feeling as though he stood out like a man wearing a bathing suit at a black tie affair, he breathed deeply, tried to calm his nerves and trusted that the dogs would not attack someone so obviously riddled with fear.

It was after four o'clock p.m. The door opened to reveal a kid wearing just an old pair of filthy-looking boxer shorts. The boy could not have been more than five years old. When he saw Troy he stepped back and let him wander inside.

Troy's nervousness grew with each step he took into the house. He wanted to leave so badly, but he knew he was there to start laying a foundation for the relationship he hoped would follow. He was there to build trust, nothing less.

Moving through the house, which was darker on the inside than he imagined it would be from the outside—the thick slabs of dark material keeping out both the sunlight and fresh air—Troy found a handful of other kids. All of them were in some state of undress, most of them wearing not much more than boxer shorts.

Eventually he found Little Ninja, similarly half dressed and unsupervised. "Hey," he said. "How are you?"

Silence.

"Did you remember I was coming to hang out with you today?"

Silence.

It wasn't the first time Troy and Little Ninja had met.

Troy had spent the previous few weeks observing him in kindergarten, and even though it was obvious that the feeling was not mutual, he felt like he knew him well already. He liked the way Little Ninja was able to focus all his attention on whatever task was ahead of him, as well as the way he could break out of his routine at a moment's notice and make a neat observation about the color of Troy's shoes or the right way to line chips up inside a sandwich.

People already knew there was something special about Little Ninja. After all, no one gets named something like Little Ninja without standing out from the pack. He had been christened Estefan, but not all that long after he learned how to talk, he developed a penchant of correctly predicting future events. It wasn't spooky or anything too out of the ordinary, but he did once call out from the back of the car, "We're going to crash," as they sped along a mountain road. Within an hour, that's exactly what happened.

Troy knew not to be too bothered by Little Ninja's shyness. Accepting a Friend into your life when you're six years old is a big step to take, especially when both parents have already completely vanished from your life.

Squatting next to Little Ninja in the hallway, Troy thought about striking up a conversation with him about the other kids in the house. Little Ninja was one of twelve, though only two of them were his siblings. He and his sisters had moved in when both of his parents were incarcerated. They had been offered a home by a family friend: a welcoming and generous single mother with a big heart and an already crowded house.

Like most of the others, Little Ninja slept on the floor and had to provide his own entertainment. As a poor boy whose parents were in prison, living in a house that struggled under the weight of poverty, growing up in a neighborhood that was increasingly dominated by gang-related activity, Little Ninja was clearly at risk. Yet with a Friend in his life to nurture his natural talents and help him make wise choices, he just might make it.

Troy and Little Ninja were due to spend an hour together on that first visit, and though he felt out of place and more than a little uncomfortable at first, once the minutes ticked silently by between them, Troy relaxed. Little Ninja did, too, and he started to point out the assorted children and recite their names. "Jungle Cat...Mr. Slushy...Princess Leia."

"Great names." said Troy, smiling. "How did they get them?"

Little Ninja looked at him directly for the first time, his face scrunched in confusion, as if the question was somehow either extremely dumb or unbearably difficult.

The two sat back, leaning up against the wall, peering into

the half darkness of the stale-aired house, watching the games play out before their eyes. They made an odd couple. But it was the beginnings of a happy couple, too.

"Starsky...Hutch...Jazz Hands..."

In time Little Ninja's shyness thawed enough for Troy to witness an emergent stronger desire; a hunger for a meaningful connection with an adult. Yes, Little Ninja was quiet and a little awkward and really quite lonely, but as he began to talk more, Troy saw within him a streak of courage, and the first shoots of determination.

It started when Troy happened to be in Little Ninja's class one day toward the end of first grade. It was sharing circle time, and the question of the day was, "What's hard in life?"

"It's hard for me to get to school on time," Little Ninja said. "I have to get my younger sister dressed and off to school first."

It was the first time that either Troy or his teacher had heard of this. They both looked at each other knowingly. It was obvious to everyone that Little Ninja had potential, but his progress had always been limited by his attendance. He had picked up forty-eight tardies so far in first grade.

Every teacher told Troy the same story: "He does well when he's here, but he can't excel because he's always late."

Troy's plan presented itself in an instant. He knew he had to be early or at least on time for every appointment with Little Ninja, but there were some practical issues that needed to be overcome as well. So he took Little Ninja to the store and told him to pick out an alarm clock. He taught him how to set it up and find a radio station that he liked, then he taught him how to tell the time. He showed him how to put the batteries in to make sure that the alarm would still work if it got unplugged in the night, and he taught him how to make a plan that would allow enough time for all the tasks that needed to be done in the morning.

The first grade ended well, with the tardies dropping off almost completely. Second grade wasn't such a great start, but Troy came up with a plan that worked perfectly. "Little Ninja," he said, "I'm going to get to your school ten minutes early tomorrow morning. And I'm going to have donuts with me. I hope you make it, 'cause your classmates are going to be eating whether you're there or not." That was pretty much the last of the tardies.

As the years passed, Troy shifted the focus of their conversations away from the practical toward the philosophical. "I wonder why so many people like going to McDonald's?" he mused as they drove by the golden arches.

The simple question would be enough to set Little Ninja's mind off on a quest to unravel the reason for the chain's popularity, and Troy would listen to the free flow of words that followed. "I guess it tastes good...it's nice to eat with other people who are happy...but I once saw a kid crying because he didn't like the clown...I don't like clowns that much either, but I like burgers more...sometimes you can stop feeling worried or scared if you really need to...but sometimes you can't because it's just too hard...but if you practice at it, you can get better at it...so maybe that kid just hadn't had as much practice at concentrating on good things as I have..."

In time, the questions came from Little Ninja himself:

"How come you went to college, Troy, but no one in my family ever did?"

"How come you have a nice car but none of the cars in my yard drive?"

"How come you chose to be a Friend?"

With every question came a stream of words. Troy enjoyed observing Little Ninja's values being shaped, watching him as his character formed in the passenger seat beside him.

Once Little Ninja reached fifth grade, Troy passed him on to a new Friend. By seventh grade, Little Ninja's GPA was a 4.0.

Just as Friends like Troy worked with kids like Little Ninja—inching their way forward, building a foundation for life out of alarm clocks and batteries, discussions about burgers and cars—Friends of the Children grew and thrived and inched its own way toward success. As it did so, the process of honing became clearer. It did not require a one-size-fits-all approach, and it did not need to become an inflexible program in which Friends worked from a script and children were guided through a syllabus. Honing meant supporting the Friends as they learned the best ways of guiding their children toward a better future. It meant being flexible, creative, patient. It meant being okay with starting small, valuing the baby steps that were needed in order to move forward.

CHAPTER 12

HARD KNOCKS, HARD LESSONS

"I'm living the dream," he told Javier. "I'm living the dream."

An old maxim says that there's a certain point in life at which a window closes. These moments are not the end in themselves, but they mark the point at which defeat becomes almost inevitable. Like the final buzzer that sounds once a team has lost the first three games in a seven game series, success is not impossible, but there's a mountain to climb in order to reach it.

In life, as in sports, people often find that they face these moments more than once. A relationship sours, an economy tanks, or a client backs off and suddenly they find themselves staring at a picture that is far bleaker than they ever hoped it would be. So they learn to make the most of these windows of opportunity before they close. Faced with unpleasant odds if they fail to act, people dig deep for all the strength and resilience within.

For many of the poorest, most vulnerable children in the United States, these windows work a little differently. They come along less often and close far quicker than they do for those with wealth, stability and opportunity. For many of the children, the last chance they get to change the course of their lives often closes off once they start first grade. At around the same time they learn to tie their shoes, millions of children living among poverty, violence, and neglect are unaware of the fact that their chance of taking hold of their own lives is slipping through their fingers.

The founders of Friends of the Children knew all this when they first started. It was the driving force behind their decision to start observing very young kids, preparing them to come into the program when they reached the end of kindergarten.

Nothing sharpens the focus of an organization quite like the realization that, for many of the people they had set out to help, they really were the last hope. So, as the years moved by and the program grew from its initial total of three Friends and twenty-four children, Duncan and his growing team of dedicated staff subtly changed the way the organization worked.

The selection process was refined to a point where one or two highly experienced Friends spent six weeks observing all the potential children who were identified by teachers. The Friends gathered evidence wherever they could find it: kids' comments and classwork, conversations with teachers, specialists, counselors, administrators, caseworkers and even playground interactions.

If the potential children volunteer information, that is well and good, but the organization never wanted children going home and saying that a stranger had been asking who they live with, or if there's enough to eat at home. Too many families have had bad experiences with state agencies, and Friends wanted to make it clear they were there to help the children, not to punish or judge a family. Friends are respectful of families, period.

Nothing is left to chance or whim. Risk factors are recorded and ranked, behavior is charted and logged, and tough questions are asked, like whether a child is beyond the scope of the program. Is there a significant, supportive adult in their lives who fulfills the role of a Friend already? Is this the kind of kid who could become successful regardless, or was he or she destined to stay at the bottom of the pile? Is the child a part of the unreachable, untouchable generation of kids that society struggles so much to help?

Of all the hard truths that Friends of the Children had to absorb, the hardest was the fact that not every child who makes it into the program will see it through to completion. The decision to leave is only ever made by the child or the parent—Friends of the Children will never kick a kid off the program; their commitment is unconditional. In fact, Friends of the Children has continued to work with an older child even though he or she has moved hundreds of miles away. Of course, sometimes a child's family move will be largely positive, bringing a fresh start and making a clean break from a difficult past. And yet, for others, the premature ending of their involvement in the program only rubs salt in wounds.

But worse than all that are the times when the chaos and cruelty of the streets win out, and a child who has slipped away from the program is killed. And though this has only happened three times in the more than two decades since Friends of the Children began, there is no pain quite as deep as the knowledge that a child has become a victim of the violence of the streets.

Those victims have names. Jason. Khalid. Darren. And despite the fact that the window of opportunity appeared to be open for all of them, the plain truth is that their chances of making it out of the streets alive were already horribly thin.

At first it seemed like Jason was one of the lucky ones. He had made it through selection into the program, and his natural talent for math and reading began to shine. His verbal skills were equally impressive, and there was plenty of talk about him as a potential lawyer. But it was his smile that got everyone   talking. When he flashed it there was little anyone could do to resist.

But in seventh grade, something changed for Jason. He started hanging out with a bad crowd in his neighborhood; he started to use that smile and those verbal powers for different purposes. Instead of winning people over with his natural innocent charm, he became more combative.

Bit by bit, he drifted away, leaving the program. The power of life with the gang was too strong for him to resist, and eventually—perhaps almost inevitably—his words got the better of him. He ran down the wrong person. One afternoon on a street corner not far from the offices of Friends of the Children, Jason was shot.

As so often happens when there is a death of a family member of a child who has been involved in Friends of the

Children, the Friends were some of the first to be called. So when Jason was shot, his former Friends were called. They rushed to the hospital. When they arrived, they found that without the machines that kept his body breathing he would be dead.

Jason's death changed things for Friends of the Children. Just as Troy's work with Little Ninja kick-started an initiative to make sure all of the children in the program were taught how to deal with the practical aspects of life—like getting up on time—so also Jason's death left its own legacy. It led to a change in the way Friends interacted with their children.

Even though it was a little hard to admit it at the time, the way Friends worked with younger kids was not necessarily the right way to work with teenagers. Adolescents want more than just parental figures. They want peers. Across the program, Friends were finding that when their teenagers were tempted to join up with local gangs, the one-on-one Friend model just didn't seem to have quite the same appeal as it did a year or so earlier.

And so, after a thorough process of self-examination, the decision makers within the program decided a change was in order.

When children became teenagers, they were transitioned to a new Friend who, instead of having eight children, would now have up to twelve teenagers. Instead of carrying out the bulk of their activities one-on-one, the new Friend encouraged all those in his care to team up and join him or her on outings. The adolescents continued to spend time with their Friend while also fulfilling their need to belong to a group of peers.

The story of Friends of the Children is one of real lives lived out against a backdrop of poverty and violence, with limited escape routes. Sometimes there are just too many factors dragging a child away.

That's how it was with Khalid.

Like all the other children accepted into the program, Khalid was exposed to enough risk factors to cause his teachers real concern. His parents had emigrated from Nigeria, and between his neighborhood and his lack of parental engagement, he was at high risk of gang involvement.

His Friend worked hard with him, attending school discipline meetings where the subject of Khalid's inappropriate behavior toward female students was often discussed. He also supported Khalid when he was kicked out of school. But when his parents decided to send their son back to Nigeria after just two years in the program, everyone at Friends of the Children feared they would not see him again.

Yet, at age twelve, he returned to Portland and rejoined the program. Even though the new way of working with adolescents was in play, Khalid drifted. And when his Friend stopped working for the program there was a four-month period during which he drifted still further away. Again, just as it had been with Jason, Khalid became involved in local gang activity.

The phone call came one afternoon. Khalid's sister was also in the program, and it was her Friend, Miss Nancy, who was the first from Friends of the Children to find out. "It's Khalid," the little girl said over the phone, between sobs. "He's dead."

It took some time to decipher what had happened, but eventually the whole story became clear. Khalid was traveling on the train with some other members of his gang. Together they were targeting a member of another gang; just a boy really, and Khalid—himself only fifteen—was carrying two weapons with him. When they approached their would-be victim, the attack didn't go according to plan. Khalid was disarmed and killed with his own weapon.

The reality for those living in poverty in America—particularly boys—is that gang-related activity is hard to resist. A Friend can be the deciding factor, can keep boys like Robert so focused and engaged that gang life never really catches their eye. But for others, such as Jason and Khalid, once they gain a taste of what it's like to belong, it can be almost impossible to back away.

Javier, the same Friend who cheered Robert on to his greatest victory on the long, gruelling STP bicycle ride, understood the way the windows of opportunity work. He'd seen them hold open for boys like Robert and close all too quickly for kids like Jason. And sometimes, just sometimes, he'd seen them sneak open again at the most unlikely of times.

While Robert remains a poster child for mentoring, Ben always seemed destined for jail. He lacked Robert's charm and self-confidence, and his face was always set in a rigid frown as if he anticipated some incoming abuse or attack.

From the beginning of first grade, he was getting into the kind of trouble normally reserved for older kids. Like many kids in the program, he slept on a couch; he never had a bed of his own, let alone a whole bedroom. Once he finished sixth grade, he pretty much dropped out of school, despite the best efforts of everyone in Friends to get him to go back. Javier tried to keep the relationship going, picking up Ben and bringing him to activities with other teens.

More than once, Ben was nursing an injury as he slumped into Javier's car. "What happened to your hand?" Javier asked one day as Ben struggled to attach his seatbelt with a heavily bandaged hand.

"There was a guy in the park last night."

"Okay," said Javier, inviting him to keep going. After too much silence, eventually the young kid got the hint.

"He was Russian. He tried to stab me. So I beat him up."

"What time did this happen?" Javier asked. "Did anyone see?"

"No. It was too dark. I think it was about three o'clock a.m."

"Three? Ben, you're only just sixteen. What are you doing out at three in the morning?"

Ben looked at Javier and shrugged. "What else am I going to do?"

The inevitable happened within a few months. Ben was caught, charged, and sentenced to seven years for armed robbery. It was a tough sentence, and as Javier visited Ben in the juvenile detention center soon after the trial, he thought that Ben had never looked younger.

"Javier," he said, his voice low, staring at his hands, "by the time I get out you won't be my Friend."

"I'll ride it out," said Javier. "I won't abandon you."

A couple of times a year Javier took a day to drive down

to southern Oregon, where Ben was incarcerated.

For the first time ever, Ben started talking about his life, how it had been before he was arrested. "My life was so chaotic," he recalled, "but whenever you came over I felt like it was normal, even if it was for just that one day."

"You know," Javier said just before he left one day, "the idea of going away for seven years sounds bad, but you're alive. And you didn't kill anyone. You get to figure out who you are while you're in here, get an education, reorient yourself, and figure out what you want life to be like when you get out. That's the gift you've been given."

Though he was serving a long sentence for a crime he had committed as a teenager who was caught up in gang-related violence, Ben managed to do what almost nobody else is ever able to do; he turned his life around. He got a high school diploma while he was in prison, graduating at the head of his class. He gave a commencement speech that made Javier's heart swell with pride and his eyes run with tears.

And when Ben was eventually released, his life was guided by different tracks than the ones that had gotten him into trouble in the first place. He found a job, fell in love, married, and became a father.

From time to time, he allowed himself a moment to take stock of all he had and the chaos he'd avoided. "I'm living the dream," he told Javier. "I'm living the dream."

We all have windows of opportunity, but just passing through them does not guarantee success. Likewise, when they seem to be shut and bolted against us, sometimes—just sometimes—there's a chance that someone can turn his or her life around.

Success isn't always easy to measure in Friends of the Children. Yes, there are compelling statistics that prove how effective and efficient the program is, numbers that show how great Friends of the Children is at keeping kids out of the Juvenile Justice System. But even among the kids who don't manage to resist the gravitational pull of crime, there are stories like Ben's, tales of triumph snatched from the jaws of defeat, glorious examples of a life where the script of generational poverty was ripped up and entirely rewritten.

CHAPTER 13

THE PROOF'S IN THE PROCESS

"What he created in Portland could change the way this country tries to help children."

D uncan was tearing up even before the night began. Just walking into the parking lot of the Friends of the Children offices was enough to leave him momentarily speechless as he held back the tears. The lot was covered by a tent large enough to park a dozen school buses and lined with chairs waiting for the descent of hordes of smiling family, friends, and supporters. Duncan checked the inside of his suit again for his notes, knowing there was a good chance he would be too emotional to use them. Soon the place would be full of people celebrating not the work of Duncan Campbell or even that of the Friends. People were coming to cheer and clap and cry tears of delight over the children themselves. This was their night and no one else's.

It was graduation night at Friends of the Children, a time to celebrate the end of a twelve-year journey, and the beginning of a whole new adventure. The seats were full long before the evening was due to start, and when Duncan stood in front of the crowd and invited the graduates to come up onto the stage, the applause was as loud as it was long.

People listened as one by one the graduates were introduced: Eddie, Victor, and Nicky. Each of them had a story to tell that could unleash even more tears, but this was not a night so much for looking back and reflecting on the troubles the children had faced. Instead, it was about the strength they had shown, the strength they had discovered and nurtured within them. It was about their futures more than it was about their pasts.

"People say I came from a bad neighborhood," Eddie said. He was a powerfully built young man who grasped the lectern with both hands and looked every inch like the quarterback that the college football programs had shown such interest in. "To me, all I knew was that ten-block radius in Northeast Portland. That was my world.

"Then Drew became my Friend. He took me to a lot of movies, a lot of lunches. He started showing me there were things other than what I knew, things I never knew existed. Like downtown, like the mountains, like sports. And all of that became a part of me, such a big part that now I've got a scholarship to go to college and play football."

Eddie looked out into the audience, found Drew, and paused. "'Thank you' doesn't sound like a big enough way to express my gratitude for what you've given me, but every bit of me means it when I say it."

Others stood up and said a few words. Some talked about the fun things they'd done with their Friends, others talked about the tough times that their Friends had helped them through. For Victor, even if the speeches went on all night he knew he would struggle to say all that he wanted to say.

He wanted to tell everyone everything about his life. He wanted to tell them how he and his mom never got along, how she blamed him for everything that went wrong in the house. She gave him so many chores he called himself Cinderfella, which made him smile just a little. He wanted to tell them about all the things she used to say as well, like how his long-gone dad was evil, how he had abused him and his two older brothers and one younger sister. And he wanted to tell them all about how, when he was old enough to start working a summer job, his mom always confiscated his paycheck, telling him that it was money he owed her anyway.

But instead of all that, he stood up and machine-gunned his words out as fast as they entered his head. "The first thing I remember about my Friend Jack was that I was goofing off in kindergarten one day, wondering why this weird guy was watching me. Then I got home and he was there, too, which really freaked me out. But Mom said, 'This is Jack, and he's going to be in your life for a while,' and Jack said, 'Do you want to go to Chucky Cheese?' and I said, 'That's my favorite!' It was the perfect start."

He thought about explaining how his mom got worse as he got older, how she would lock him out of the house until she got home at midnight and how, when she married a martial arts expert, he feared for his safety in the house. But it was all so complicated that he thought twice. Instead he told the simplest version of his story. "I first tried to kill myself when I was twelve. I tried again when I was sixteen, and again when I was seventeen. If I didn't have a Friend, I would have kept on trying until I succeeded."

The room was quiet now, some eyes lowered, others lifted up toward Victor. "My mom tried to pull me out the program, but I fought to stay in. I went to court, spoke up for my rights and got put in foster care. I got a 3.8 my junior year, took on AP Calculus and AP English, then I won a scholarship to go to college."

Victor wondered whether he should add something to close the speech off, but there were too many people clapping and cheering already. Even if he had thought of something to say, no one would have heard him. So he just returned to his seat and felt relieved that his speech was over.

The evening grew late and there was just one last graduate to address the crowd before Duncan's closing speech. Like so many of the other graduates, Nicky had defied the odds by making it all the way through high school, securing admission to college in the fall. She had come a long way from the days of escaping the fighting at home by climbing into the safety of the thin branches of the nearby cedar trees. And though as a young child she wished that she could miraculously transport herself to adulthood, the years had taught her well. She had navigated her way through fear, though grief, and away from the caustic words that her aunt Amy dropped on her. She had come a long way, indeed.

Like the others, Nicky was feeling nervous. But she knew what she wanted to say, and she knew to whom she wanted to say it. Standing in front of the lectern, she looked out to find Matt—the man who had left his job so that she would not be separated from her siblings—as well as Jen, her most recent Friend. Her sister and brother were there, too, both radiating gigawatt smiles. Her aunt didn't think it was a big enough deal for her to travel all the way to Portland from Texas, which made Nicky happy. Her mom wanted to be there, but it would be months before there was any chance she would be released from prison.

"When I was a kid, and there was fighting at home, I used to climb trees and wish that I could be eighteen. I wanted to get my childhood over with but didn't know how it could change. Well, it changed. And I made it."

When the cheers died down, it was Duncan's turn to speak. There was no need for the notes he'd prepared. Instead, he stood at the microphone and twisted back around so that his comments would go directly to the graduates themselves.

"I've got just one thing to say to you. Not only am I proud of you, but I loved you when I met you, I love you now, and I'll love you forever."

Before the event was over, the tent taken down and the tears dried, Duncan and his team were able to process some of the data they had gained about the program. What they discovered about the impact of Friends of the Children amazed them. Even though they had known all along that lives were being changed by the work that the Friends were doing with the children, to see the figures in black and white added a whole new weight to the findings. Despite the fact that 60 percent of them had parents who dropped out of high school, 83 percent of the children graduated from high school or earned a GED. Despite 50 percent having come from homes where one parent was incarcerated, more than 93 percent of kids involved in the Friends of the Children program stayed out of the Juvenile Justice System. Although 85 percent of the children were born to a teenage parent, a colossal 98 percent avoided becoming teen parents themselves.

No wonder Gary Walker, past president of Public/Private Ventures—the social research and policy organization that was so influential in the rise of Big Brothers Big Sisters of America in the 1990s—declared that what was going on in Portland was worth noticing.

"In my professional life, I've seen only a few programs that I think have a shot at really making a difference. I don't casually toss around words like *brilliant* and *unique*, but what Duncan Campbell did is brilliant and unique. What he created in Portland could change the way this country tries to help children."

***

AT THE SAME TIME FRIENDS OF THE CHILDREN began to thrive, so Campbell Global began operating at full strength. By the time the program started holding annual graduation ceremonies, the company had grown substantially.

The money was useful, allowing Duncan to support the work of Friends of the Children in Portland, but he knew that the problems he wanted to tackle needed far more money than any individual could provide. What Friends of the Children needed was to export the model to other cities.

As was so often the case, Duncan found that the key to making this happen was already close at hand. And, as was also the case, the solution presented itself while he was out among the pines, the firs, and the cedar trees that cover so much of Oregon.

He was hiking at Black Butte, an idyllic spot near the high Cascade Mountains just a couple of hours southeast of Portland. With him was Doug Stamm, a fellow lawyer who was ten years his junior and headed up Nike's community affairs program. They'd met years before at a community meeting that focused on children's issues in Oregon, becoming fast friends. Doug saw Duncan as a role model and mentor, both in business and in community work.

Together they hiked up the steep path that wove between aging ponderosa pines that wore their orange bark like cracked leather armor, and smelled of butterscotch and vanilla. Far below them the forest spread out for miles, and as they climbed, their conversation turned to the subject of Doug's career.

"When I was in college," he said, "serving in the Peace Corps was a big deal, but I never did anything like that. I went from being a trial lawyer to working at Nike. Now I'm wondering whether it's time I gave back to the community."

Even today, hiking is Duncan's preferred aid to creative thinking. As the two men crossed a treeless slope lined with white flowers, he asked Doug, "What do you think you're good at? What are you good at building?"

"I love building programs," Doug said.

"Okay. Well, I need someone to build my program. I want to replicate what's happening in Portland. I want to take it national."

The men passed by other wildflowers, great blankets of yellow, purple, and red that fell back as the path climbed sharply again. Duncan kept talking though, telling Doug he recognized his own mortality. "I want the program to live on. I need to position strong people to run it. I've lived two very different lives—a menace on the streets and the world of successful business—and I know that's useful and unique. But while I can make it happen in Portland, I can't bottle it up and take it out across the country. That's not my skill. But you, Doug…you can."

Any nonprofit leader can tell you that replicating a unique program isn't easy. Most of the organizations that make it through infancy do so because of the influence of a charismatic visionary founder like Duncan who develops a team around them. The visionary dictates the culture of the organization and keeps watch over it as it grows and evolves. It all works well on a small scale, but when organizations try to replicate the program with new people in new places, it often creates new obstacles.

Doug knew Duncan well already. He knew he had a lot of moving parts, that the influence of his childhood had given him both a tremendous resilience and a deep need for strong relationships. Was he willing to let go of the organization enough to allow others to take it on?

And then there was the organization itself. While some

saw replication as a matter of following a business model, where the blueprints and scripts had to be followed line by line, Doug knew that a program like Friends of the Children could not be franchised like a donut store. He intuitively understood that it was far more like a house: it had to be custom built to preexisting plans from the ground up in its new location.

If someone was going to successfully replicate Friends of the Children's way of dealing with the most at-risk children, making it work in other cities, he or she would be facing a steep climb. But Doug instinctively knew it would be worth it.

By the time the top of the butte crept into sight, Duncan made Doug an offer. By the time they reached the summit, Doug said yes.

PART THREE

TALL TREES
IN
NEW YORK CITY

CHAPTER 14

PS241, HARLEM

"Everybody in the city is at risk. There's no shame in doing something about that, is there?"

I t was hot on the morning of 2001 when Duncan headed toward 115th street in New York City, looking for a certain door that he'd been unable to locate. The humidity sapped him of energy. The way the buildings were stacked tightly against each other shielded the streets below from any cooling breeze. Central Park was just a short walk south, and he liked the idea of sitting in the shade of a tree and watching the city dwellers go about their business. Still, he was here to visit the new offices of the latest chapter to emerge in the Friends of the Children family. A little physical discomfort had no chance of dampening his excitement.

As he rounded the corner on 115th, Duncan passed by the liquor store. Lying on their backs outside in the mid-afternoon sun were two customers who, as they did almost every afternoon, had decided to park it for a few hours and sleep off the booze.

Had he lingered a while and looked around him, Duncan would have seen various other sights typical of Harlem and other parts of the five New York boroughs. Hand-to-hand transactions made in the blink of an eye, dark vans with blacked out windows pausing outside, looking ominous, as police poured out of the vehicle and clambered up the steps.

But there has always been more to Harlem than drunks, drug deals, and police raids. The arrival of spring always brings people out onto the sidewalk, standing in stark contrast to winter where it sees that half the population remains in hibernation. As the air warms, so does the need to escape the stale indoor air. Car shops, barbershops, and all other trades in between routinely move their business outside. Hijacked fire hydrants still offer relief to those kids wanting to play in their jets, and the usual spread of street games—basketball, chess, and card games like Pitty Pat and poker—all take place on the sidewalks and streets.

Eventually, having passed by a couple of times, Duncan found what he was looking for: a battered blue metal door. While the chapter back in Portland had moved into an old Catholic school at which the entrance hall sat behind tall doors designed to invite students in, the blue metal door was designed for other purposes. 115th was a long way from the leafy residential road that was home to the Portland chapter.

Since Doug Stamm started working for Friends of the Children, new chapters came thick and fast. First there was Seattle, then San Francisco, but to be here in New York City was an opportunity too good to resist. And whenever Duncan got the chance to visit with the people in New York, he took it.

New York needed—and still needs—Friends of the Children. For all its improvements over the years, for all the sliding crime figures and its high profile community programs, certain parts of the city are still risky places for children to grow up. And in order to begin to properly understand what life is like for those that the latest Friends of the Children chapter set out to help, a little history is required.

By many accounts, the 1980s were the years when New York was at its most authentic, vibrant, and unshackled. The city was untamed and unapologetic, the ultimate urban jungle. The subway cars were the city's sketchpad, the high-rises its places of refuge and escape, the streets its dance floor. For others, the 1980s were a decade best forgotten. Lined in yellow tape, cordoned off by geography, at times it felt as if the entire city was on the losing side of a battle against drugs, gangs, and crime that ranged from little more than petty and of the street variety to highly organized and even international. The city was violent, often looking more like a war zone than a capital of contemporary culture. And for a whole generation of children, it was home.

Harlem suffered the most, just as it always had. In the 1960s, residents of Harlem were ten times more likely to be drug addicts than residents of other parts of New York City. They were also six times more likely to be murdered. By the time the 1980s came around, the drug epidemic that started with heroin in the 1960s eventually gave way to a new danger: crack. Those who could get away from Harlem did so. In fact, the exodus from the city's toughest neighborhoods had started years before. Middle class families, mainly African-American, moved out to the nicer suburbs in Queens, the Bronx, and lower Westchester. Those that remained were the ones who simply could not afford to go elsewhere.

The poor were left behind, like refugees from an unwanted tribe. Drugs and drug dealers ruled from 110th up to 168th, and lawlessness ensued. Crack changed things on the streets, especially when it came to the types of crimes that were committed. In the pre-crack days of the early 1980s, the vulnerable were getting stuck up by the tough guys in the neighborhood. Sneakers, coats, and cash were all on the menu for the street robber. But once they graduated to selling crack, they left behind petty street crime. Soon, the only guys attempting to rob people down there on the streets were the crackheads themselves. In their weakened state, they were a good deal less intimidating than the purse snatchers of yore.

While robbery eased a little, things at the other end of the scale got steadily and dramatically worse. In 1985 there were 1,683 reported murders in New York City. In 1990 that number had increased to 2,605—a record that still stands today[3]. As more people became addicted to crack, so crime rates increased.

For a while, Harlem was America's dirty little secret, a wound everyone knew existed but no one chose to address. The 1980s were tough times, and while Friends of the Children was yet to emerge in conversation between Duncan and Orin, this decade remains a crucial time for anyone interested in the lives of young people living two and three

[3] source: http://www.disastercenter.com/crime/nycrime.htm

decades later. Why? Because among the violence and the addiction, among the lack of prospects and the stench of decay, a generation of children were struggling out of infancy toward adolescence. And when they started to have babies, many of them didn't have the faintest idea how to be an adult, let alone how to be a parent.

One of the most significant facts about the 1980s was the way crack impacted the lives of the women and girls. The previous drugs of choice that accompanied other decades— booze, cocaine, heroin—were more likely to snare men, but crack was different. Women became hooked, with terrible results.

Previously, with their husbands and boyfriends strung out on drugs, drunk, or in jail, it had fallen on the women to provide for their families. However, once crack got its hands on them, everything changed. Many turned to prostitution in an effort to keep themselves supplied, and those who had children were largely incapable of providing either emotionally or physically in any significant way for their children.

And so, a new generation of children was slowly introduced to the monstrous city. They had little or no contact with their fathers, and their mothers were just as likely to be absent in one way or another. Some of the kids were taken in by their grandmothers, others were fostered, and those who fell through the cracks were left to fend for themselves. Nearly all of them felt the pull of the streets, where their peers ran unsupervised, embracing trouble in all its forms.

For Duncan, the need for Friends of the Children here

was obvious. The only question was whether the system that had worked so well in Portland—and which was beginning to work elsewhere—would work in the most depraved part of the country. Harlem was a long, long way from the West Coast, in many ways.

Having discussed how to replicate the model, Duncan and Doug decided that the best chances of success would come when new chapters were pioneered by a local champion capable of developing strong relationships with others. The program itself thrived when it built long term, nurturing relationships with vulnerable children, so it made sense that any new chapter would have to be led by an individual with the appetite and the skills to build strong relationships with others. Plus, there was the money issue. Getting people to accept and support a project was going to be a whole lot easier if the community felt understood and well served by the people who ran it.

Friends of the Children, New York City chapter, started with all this and more. Howard Clyman, a long time friend of Friends of the Children's first executive director Mike Forzley, had moved to Brooklyn. Howard had seen Friends of the Children in action in Portland, and he and his wife, Kathie Roberts, were convinced that this move was a unique opportunity to make an impact in the lives of children who were growing up in some of the worst parts of the country. They were committed to founding the chapter. Given that Kathie had been a judge on the federal bench, and Howard was an attorney, their chances of success were good from the outset.

In 2001, having moved home to Brooklyn and taken the first steps to getting Friends of the Children New York registered and functioning as an independent nonprofit, they started the work of establishing themselves among the community. It was a crowded space with great need—a place that required an enormous amount of funding and a large number of organizations clambering for finite resources.

As Howard researched and sought advice from NYC nonprofit providers of youth services, he was referred by Doug Stamm to the Pinkerton Foundation, a potential source of funding that had been on his radar. Howard went to Pinkerton's beautiful office at Rockefeller Center to meet with Executive Director Joan Colello, whom he found to be receptive—thanks to the fact that she had already visited Friends in Portland, and had come away impressed. Joan and Pinkerton granted seed money to begin a Friends chapter in New York, including funds for the initial search for a partner school site. Understanding Friends of the Children's approach and values, Pinkerton suggested that Howard explore a particular school in Harlem, which eventually became the school in which the chapter began. It was the start of a significant relationship within the New York program's story, as Pinkerton remained a steadfast supporter over the coming years. The board eventually voted to name the Friend's House in Harlem after Joan.

While wealthy middle class white folks pledging to change the lives of the poor for the better was nothing new, there was enough about what Howard, Kathie, and the Friends were offering that got people to listen. Other groups talked about their program. Howard, Kathie, and the Friends talked about the children. Others presented a timetable of results delivered over a period of months, while from the outset Friends of the Children was clear that any child in the program would probably not see significant improvement in their grades for at least four or five years. Other programs brought in experts and specialists from outside, while the Friends were all experienced in working with children who had grown up in New York neighborhoods—just like the community they hoped to serve.

What little resistance they met was based on numbers and language. Following the Portland model, once children had been selected, the parents were all invited in to discuss the program and go through the paperwork. It was often there, in the small group setting, that the questions emerged. "Why can't you take both of my kids?" some parents asked. "And why is mine being selected in the first place? Are they bad? Is there something wrong with them? Does this mean they're in special education now?"

These same questions had been raised back in Portland, too, especially the one about enrolling only one child. Just as in the original project, the New York chapter was there for the most at-risk children. If one sibling was accepted into the program and another was not, it was only ever because the risk factors were different for the two children. These were never easy conversations to have, especially with a mother who is already overwhelmed by life. As a result, the New York chapter moved away from working through the paperwork in a small group setting, choosing instead to go through it in a face to face meeting with the individual parents themselves. The more direct and honest the Friends were, and the more space the parents had to ask questions and work through the answers, the easier it was for them to accept the idea.

In those early days it often fell to Kareem Wright, a man who seemed unable to walk into a school playground without being surrounded and climbed onto by a sizeable crowd of children, some enrolled in the program, others not. As one of the earliest and longest-serving Friends in the program, Kareem was called on to help explain things more clearly. He had grown up in the city and knew the people and the risks, as well as the way to break free of the dangers. He used phrases such as, "Your child has promise," or, "We've chosen her because she has potential." It was his hope to encourage the parents and guardians to focus on the positive side of things instead of getting sidetracked by any sense of anger or embarrassment. Everything he said was true, but in time he, as well as the other Friends, learned that parents and guardians responded better when they were given the whole truth straight up.

So, when asked by a parent why a child was being offered a place, Kareem told him or her what he had seen during the six-week observation period: the good as well as the bad. "Is your child at risk?" Kareem said. "Yes, they are. But so was I when I was a teen. Everybody in the city is at risk. There's no shame in doing something about that, is there?"

Despite the confusion and complexity of New York's school system, Friends of the Children kept it simple at first, working with just one school, PS241, on 113th. In year two they added another two Friends, including Kareem. As a former teacher, Kareem told Howard and the first program manager, Margot Tenenbaum, during his interview that he was very proud to be a product of NYC schools, from kindergarten through his BA at Brooklyn College.

"Whenever I'm in a school setting I always carry a book under my arm so the children will understand the importance of reading," he told them. Kareem was happy to make the transition from leading a classroom of thirty kids to making a meaningful, long-term connection with eight. Like the other Friends, he spent a lot of time in PS241, taking his kids out of the classroom at agreed times and working with them in another room. With between 400 and 500 children enrolled in the school, the five Friends, each with eight kids they were assigned to mentor, made a dramatically positive impact not just on the children themselves, but on the whole school.

As Duncan stood on the street by the blue metal door, he was buzzed in. He shut the door carefully behind him and descended the spiral stairs, enclosed in a wire screen, that led down to the basement. It was his first time in the new office. He took in the scene: low ceilings, no natural light, a warren of open spaces flowing from one to the other. It was a long way from the kind of offices successful lawyers, entrepreneurs, even teachers would have aspired to. Yet, the fabric of the building wasn't what stood out most. Instead, it was the noise and the people that made the biggest impression on Duncan. For there in front of him, filling out the space with their laughter, their photos plastered over the walls, were the children. Among them were the Friends—

talking, laughing, sitting at small tables and working side by side with their kids. It was perfect.

Out of nowhere, a man almost twelve inches taller, but with a smile just as bright as Duncan's, appeared at his side. "Kareem!" Duncan said. His hand extended for a fist bump, which was then followed with a hug.

"Mr. Duncan," Kareem said, stepping aside. "I've got someone I'd like you to meet." From behind him emerged a skinny little boy with wide eyes and feet that looked two sizes too big for his little legs. "Tony, say hi to Mr. Campbell."

CHAPTER 15

KIDS, THE REAL HEROES

"All of us have assets and liabilities, and it just depends which one is going to outweigh the other."

Kareem looked at Duncan and nodded toward his child, Tony, as he began. "I was just talking with Tony here about what he'd do if he was ever asked by someone to take an envelope up to 135th street. Tell Mr. Duncan what you told me, Tony."

Though he was yet to grow into his feet, Tony was one of those confident thirteen-year-old boys whose personality was already far bigger than his physical imprint. He had an easy smile, and a voice that was slow enough to show that he believed people would listen to what he had to say.

Tony spoke in a measured tone. "I said that people started asking me to do that kind of thing when I was nine years old."

Kareem looked at Duncan. "The gangs are recruiting kids younger and younger these days. If people are offering you envelopes to run down the block at nine, you have to grow up quickly. You don't get to enjoy being nine like other kids do. So we're learning that we have to start these conversations far earlier than we did when the program first began."

While Portland suffered some gang activity, it was nothing like New York. The days of mafia dons with their elaborate chains of command were long gone. In their place had emerged a new type of career criminal, the teenage gangbanger. Too young to drink, vote or even to drive, their lives were often as short as they were violent. These children of fourteen and fifteen years old had few of the instincts for self-preservation that their older predecessors had, and their world was more violent as a result.

"Tell Mr. Duncan what you said to me about those people who asked you to run that envelope for them."

"I said, 'Never that.'"

Duncan shot a quizzical look in Kareem's direction. "It's a street term," said Kareem. "It means there's no way he'd do it."

"Why, Tony?" said Duncan.

The boy didn't need any time to think about the question. "I like girls," he said. "So there's no way I want to go to prison." With that, Tony grinned his way to the bathroom.

"Tony's a smart kid," said Kareem, watching him leave the room. "He's had that same confidence about him from a young age, and now he's strong enough to know he won't do anything just because someone tries to pressure him. But I've been concerned about him lately, especially because his brother and father were both incarcerated recently, and within a month of each other. His brother's in for five years and his dad's in for twenty. I've been wondering whether he would swerve toward the path his father and brother took or continue to enjoy his freedom. I guess the girls have decided it for him at the moment."

Both men knew it didn't always go that way, and both knew that gang life throughout New York was every bit the threat as it ever had been. Even kids who made it into the program, and appeared to be building a solid future for themselves, were at risk.

If he could, Kareem also would have introduced Duncan to Dwight. Dwight was a good kid from 128th street. He'd been in the program since he started school, but his mother was an infamous crack dealer who ruled her block with fear and absolute authority. For Dwight, the risks of gang involvement were even higher than they were for others.

The program helped, and he wanted to do right. When he was fourteen years old, he was out walking one day when he saw an armed robbery in progress. A young kid he didn't know had pinned an older looking guy up against the wall. The older one was clearly scared, waving his hands around. Dwight stepped in and stopped it. In that one moment it seemed as though a whole new path might be opening up for him, as if he was now making enough of the right kind of choices to build up some positive momentum in his life. The guy he rescued owned a restaurant. He gave Dwight a job to show his thanks, and for a few months the future looked even more secure. But when Dwight was accused of stealing from the restaurant— and was subsequently fired—he drifted away from Kareem and Friends of the Children, back toward the life that surrounded his home. He became harder: harder to find, harder for Kareem to connect with, harder to have honest conversations with about where he wanted his life to go.

Over the thirteen years of the program working in Harlem, Dwight is one of just two kids who chose to leave it. As Duncan envisioned years before, getting kicked off is simply impossible. The Friends will always make any and all adjustments necessary to accommodate whatever changes come up. For Dwight, when the calling of the streets grew to its strongest, even the sixteen hours a month Kareem spent with him could not compete. And while his mom said all the right things, encouraging her boy to go on out and enjoy the time he was spending with Kareem, whenever he was at home she did little to try to hide the drug dealing from her son.

The deeper Dwight sank into gang life, the more Kareem started to worry. Not just for Dwight either, but for the rest of the kids who saw Friends of the Children's offices as a safe, nurturing environment. With Dwight's gang connections, his increased risk, and the level of gang activity already at play in the streets around the offices, the staff began to worry. Kareem made the difficult decision to ask Dwight not to come to the offices anymore, suggesting instead that the two meet up elsewhere. Eventually, Dwight backed out of the program altogether.

Kareem's phone rang at two o'clock a.m. not long after Dwight had backed away from him. "I'm locked up," he said, "and I need some help." Kareem remembered the couple of times that Dwight—after some argument or other with his mom—had come to stay at his house out in New Jersey. That was back before Kareem had become a father. Was it a mistake? If Dwight's troubles now extended to jail time, had it been unwise to bring him home in those earlier times? Did Kareem in some way place his family in danger?

The story behind Dwight's arrest didn't take long to emerge. Dwight had been smoking, and he was high when he decided he was hungry. The guy at the store around the corner from his home took longer than Dwight thought was necessary to ring up his food, so he pulled out his gun and told the guy that if he didn't hurry up he'd shoot him. Dwight had barely finished his sandwich by the time the police picked him up and took him to the station. And so the prison system closed its doors behind another young African-American man whose potential had gotten lost somewhere along with his childhood.

"There's a level of self-hatred among those who get caught up in gangs," Kareem said. "So many of them hate that they're trapped in this life, but they'll eat their own, dragging others back into it to join them. If kids like Dwight want to escape, they have to be stronger. They've got to have something special about them."

When Friends of the Children set up camp in Harlem, the organization's leadership decided to call all those accepted into the program something other than kids or children. They called them Achievers. With almost half of them having a parent in jail and 80 percent living with someone other than a parent, many of them had rarely experienced anyone saying anything positive about them. Most were more likely to be told they were unwanted or worthless. To be called an Achiever reminded them, if only in a small way, that they were of value, and that their potential could begin to be fulfilled right here, right now.

If ever Kareem and the rest of the team at Friends of the Children were in doubt about the importance of the words they used to describe the program and the people they were there to help, Jazmin made it all perfectly clear. She was pretty upset at them for a while.

Jazmin lived in one of the high-rise apartment blocks that the Friends were warned not to go into alone. Between the broken elevators caked in dried urine and the drug dealers working in the hall, it simply wasn't safe for female Friends to visit their children alone.

It wasn't just the poverty or the housing that put Jazmin at risk. Her mom was critically ill and her dad was not coping well. The worse her mom got, the less time she got to spend with her. First, Jazmin needed to attend school. Then, when her mom's health worsened, Jazmin and her sister were sent to stay with her mom's best friend. The further her mom slipped away, the further Jazmin was kept from her. So she learned to cope the only way she could: with strong armor and a powerful set of weapons.

For instance, even when she was in kindergarten it was obvious that Jazmin was defiant and combative. She argued all the time, fighting her teachers on every little thing. Each day became a succession of small battles fueled by anger and hostility as Jazmin desperately tried to claw back some control in a life that was being torn away from her. She was accepted into the program, and began the process of bonding with her Friend, but even Jazmin saw herself as more of a fighter than a child.

By the time Jazmin finished third grade, her mom had passed away. Not long after that, her dad died, too, leaving her and her sister in the middle of a fierce custody battle. Though Jazmin's mom had asked a friend to promise to take care of her daughters, Jazmin's maternal grandmother had other plans. She mounted a legal challenge to require the girls to move down to rural Georgia with her. Their house was remote in the extreme, and the survivalist lifestyle, with almost zero interaction with other people, held no appeal for the grieving sisters.

The custody battle lasted more than two years, with both sides fighting tooth and nail. It was a mess, and when the case finally made it to court, emotions were running so high that the judge was forced to shout above the melee, "Everybody quiet! The only people I want to hear speaking right now are them." The judge pointed at the team from Friends of the Children, who had been by Jazmin's side throughout.

Jazmin and her sister got what they wanted. They stayed in Harlem with their guardian. Her Friend, Kayla, carried on encouraging and supporting her, and Jazmin began to develop a taste for swimming, poetry, and acting. Her academics improved, too, but the ending was far from happy. When she reached fifth grade and early adolescence, right on cue, Jazmin started to push back against the authority figures in her life. She argued with her guardian, sitting dead silent in counseling sessions. Her anger and her grief fused, only intensifying the pain and confusion she felt.

And when she Googled Friends of the Children one day, what she saw made her mad.

"Who told you I was at-risk?" she said to Kayla on the phone that day. "I'm not at-risk. There's nothing wrong with me."

Kayla knew better than to become defensive. She knew Jazmin's anger was preferable to her silence. And she also had a hunch that Jazmin was, in some way, right.

"Jazmin," she said, "you were chosen because when we looked at all the kids in your kindergarten class it was clear you had a lot of potential. But it was also clear you had a lot of things that were going to keep you from realizing that potential. You argued readily; you rejected what your teachers were saying; you didn't care much about school. But the positive side was that you spoke up for yourself. Your mom was sick. Your dad was struggling. But you had other people around you who cared. None of that stuff defines you, but it can all affect you—the good as well as the bad. All of us have assets and liabilities. It just depends which one is going to outweigh the other."

Nothing with Jazmin was fixed overnight, but she gradually allowed herself to trust Kayla again, to go a little deeper, to lean a little heavier on her. Their discussions prompted a change in the way Kareem, Kayla, and other Friends spoke with their children about the program. They would from then on talk more openly about some of the risks the kids faced, opening up some new and healthy conversations in the process. For the children attending fundraising events, sharing their stories and helping donors to put names and faces to the program, it was important that they understood that even though they would hear phrases such as "at-risk" and "incarcerated parents," none of it was a criticism of them or their families. "When people hear your story," Kareem would tell them, "they will want to do something to help others just like you."

Just as Friends of the Children has learned how to work with communities, families and the children themselves, modifying, adapting and responding to the unique challenges that each represent, so they have had to learn how to represent their work to donors. Hollywood has painted some vivid pictures of how educated, well meaning, and enlightened middle-class people can step in to an impoverished neighborhood and change things for the better. But real life does not follow the same script as *Dangerous Minds, The Blind Side, Coach Carter* or *Freedom Writers*. While we might find it easier to catch the vision of a single individual being able to heroically save at-risk kids from the projects, it misses the point. The hero is not the rookie teacher who refuses to quit, or the headstrong, straight-talking wife and mother who refuses to be beaten by injustice. The heroes—the very people who have to risk everything, who have the most to lose and who face the greatest roadblocks that only they can scale—are the children themselves. All the qualities that help them to be resilient come from within themselves. Friends of the Children simply gives them the cheerleading and guidance to help them—and their family—through.

Of course, telling it like it is becomes a far harder sell. Given a choice, wouldn't a donor much rather put their money into a project that has real life Hollywood-type heroes working for them? Wouldn't they rather bask a little in the glow of success-by-association, knowing that their dollars paid the salary of someone truly remarkable and unique? Who wants to hand over his or her money to help an undercover support worker? And who wants to invest in a program that deals with the very communities that we spend so much of our time trying to avoid and forget about?

The people who support the work of Friends of the Children are those who see beyond the headlines and who see the truth behind the movies. They're the ones who realize that nobody else works with kids like Jazmin, Dwight, and Tony. Though some people volunteer what time they can for other programs, they're not trained to work with impoverished families and they can't commit the time or the longevity to the work. Friends of the Children supporters understand that when a kid has a less than 50 percent chance of graduating high school, something unique has to be done.

Jazmin decided to work through her anger instead of letting it gnaw at her. She got involved in a program at Columbia University, coming about as close as any other child had ever come to winning a scholarship from the Posse Foundation. She did work her way to a full-ride scholarship at Syracuse University. She also landed a summer internship at an entertainment law firm, going on to becoming a regular speaker on behalf of Friends of the Children at fundraisers and award ceremonies.

Every time Jazmin climbed the steps at the side of the stage and walked toward the podium to talk about the program that changed her life, Kareem, Kayla, and a whole bunch of others were there in the crowd, cheering her on, watching the real hero in action.

CHAPTER 16

"WHY IS JESUS ALWAYS A WHITE GUY?"

"You don't have to take that path for yourself."

Having started out as one of the first Friends, Kareem progressed at Friends of the Children New York, taking on new roles and responsibilities as the years passed. Though he became Director of Programs, he continued working with a couple of children, like Elijah, with whom Kareem had started working when the program was in its second year.

His first impressions were that Elijah was a hyperactive little kid. He careened around the kindergarten classroom like a pinball. Elijah seemed to have an unfortunate fondness for taking his pants down in recess.

The rest of Kareem's observation period revealed to him a kid that was at-risk in all areas: socially, academically, emotionally, physically. He was picked on by other kids, he cried easily, he hid under desks when he thought he might be in trouble, and he had a cryptic way of smiling that portrayed both joy and sorrow at the same time. But it was not until he was formally in the program that the full story emerged.

Like other uniformed schools, students at PS241 were given two or three sets of gray pants and white T-shirts at the start of the year. It was October by the time Kareem came to observe Elijah, and his clothes were already far more stained than those of his peers. Home was obviously difficult. At least whenever Kareem arrived on a Saturday morning to get Elijah to take him down to Central Park and feed the ducks, his grandmother met him at the door downstairs.

"Let me take a photo," she said, pulling out an old camera and bustling Elijah over toward Kareem. Elijah hung his head low, as if it had gained twenty pounds overnight. "Oh, come on, will you? This is exciting."

Elijah relaxed a little on the walk to the park, and by the time he and Kareem arrived at the water he was ready to enjoy himself. He laughed at the way the ducks fought over the scraps of bread they threw for them. He tried to land as many pieces as he could on the backs of the biggest birds. After an hour or so of seeing who could throw bread the farthest and highest, they walked back to the apartment. They buzzed at the door and waited until Elijah's grandmother came down to take him in.

For months it went on the same way, every visit Kareem made starting and ending with this pantomime of prisoner exchange out in the street. Even though Kareem was sure that Elijah's grandmother was excited by the idea of Elijah being in the program, he was puzzled as to why she kept her guard up. Was she hiding something, or was she just holding Kareem at a distance, trying to remind him that he was still a stranger to them?

All Kareem knew for sure was that Elijah's mother was absent, his grandmother was nervous, and that, whenever he won a bread-throwing contest, his face lit up.

When it did come, the breakthrough was gradual.

The first step was when Kareem showed up at the apartment and buzzed, expecting the usual pause before he saw two pairs of feet descending from the stairs. Instead he heard a shout: "You should come up. He's not ready yet."

The stairwell was dark, but that was nothing compared to the inside of the apartment. Every window was covered with thick, dark sheets, and what few lights were on in the rooms were too weak to really pierce the darkness. Looking around, Kareem recognized the type of home immediately. He'd grown up in Brooklyn and seen these kinds of apartments before. There was not a single surface that was not taken up with some kind of clutter. There were piles of clothes, cooking utensils, old suitcases without handles, and miscellaneous cardboard boxes split at the side.

"Sit down," the grandmother said, before disappearing out of the room.

Kareem looked at the couch wondering where he should relocate the pile of papers that was occupying the least crowded cushion.

After that day, Kareem didn't have to wait in the street any more. Gradually he became a trusted helper, often being asked to make sure that Elijah got dressed before they went out together. And as the trust increased, Kareem was entrusted with more of the family's story.

Elijah's Mom had grown up on 112th in the dark days of

the 1980s, when crack and crime dominated Harlem. Life was full of guns, drugs, and prospects so bleak that the only way to survive was to retreat indoors. But Elijah's mom didn't do that. Instead, she hung out with the guys who carried guns and sold crack, and even before she was ten she was running numbers for them, learning how to navigate life on the streets. It was inevitable that she would become addicted to crack herself, giving birth to Elijah before she reached her sixteenth birthday.

Elijah's mom was incarcerated by the time Kareem started working with him. Elijah's biological father, so his mom said, lived a couple of blocks down, but between his drug dealing and her drug addiction, there was little chance of either of them stepping up as parents. So it fell to his grandmother to raise him.

Like a lot of women of her generation living in the city, she knew she'd failed her daughter. Bringing up her grandson Elijah was her chance to make things right, a second chance to bring up a child in the city without him winding up in jail.

She had failed to put any rules in place with her daughter, and it was clear to Kareem that she was trying to run things differently this time around. She struggled a little. Her work hours were irregular, and no matter how Kareem tried to talk to her about it, she simply couldn't see the importance of getting Elijah to bed on a regular basis, and early enough, each night.

"With or without sleep," she said, "that boy is crazy." In her mind, the main problem resided with the fact that in the times she was away at night she had no choice other than to send Elijah to sleep at his dad's place. There among the drugs and great crowd of children raised by yet another grand-mother experiencing parenthood for the second time around, Elijah stood no chance of getting any sleep at all.

The school staff wanted Elijah evaluated for mental health issues, but to Kareem it was doubtful the tests would be conclusive. In his mind, Elijah was simply reacting to the chaos of home life. Why shouldn't he act out?

Together Kareem and Elijah's grandmother started channeling the boy's energy. They walked a lot on their outings. Kareem also introduced Elijah to tae kwon do, but it was basketball that really made an impression. Elijah was instantly obsessed with the sport, happily grappling with the fundamentals, talking about it non-stop.

This opened up a whole new avenue of communication. Instead of Kareem scolding Elijah about his behavior, his bedtime, or whether or not he really had pulled his pants down again at recess, new conversations began to emerge.

"Who do you think the Knicks are gonna play next? How do you think they managed to win that last game? What makes a great player?"

Elijah responded, not with his typical one- or two-word answers, which he usually gave when talking about a teacher he didn't like or a kid who bugged him. When it came to basketball, his answers were a steady and free-flowing flood.

Soon, the questions started coming back to Kareem in reciprocation. Elijah would pick a player and obsess about him, asking Kareem "Why did he go from high school to the NBA? How many points did he get per game to be so special? What did he have to do to get that good?"

From these conversations, an awareness of the possibility of going to college dawned over the boy. Elijah soon knew which player went where, and started to form opinions about which kind of college a ball player like himself ought to consider. It drove him to practice more, to go to tournaments talking at length about the importance of skills like communication and teamwork—not just on the court, but in life.

"This is a marathon, not a sprint," Kareem reminded him on the days when he felt particularly impatient for change. "You've got to give it time." *You can't put a Band-Aid on a bullet wound,* Kareem thought.

The neighborhood of Harlem began to undergo a process of gentrification at about the same time Elijah hit a growth spurt, and the development of his basketball-themed escape plan really took off. Harlem landlords realized they could charge higher rents to the middle class professionals who had been priced out of the market elsewhere in the city, and as the police wrested control of the streets back from the crackheads and drug dealers, the worst of the poverty began to move north, toward the Bronx. And yet, with members of the Bloods gang living in his apartment block—as well as Elijah's burgeoning size—his risk of falling into gang activity was high.

When his mother was finally released from prison, and she moved back home, the honeymoon period did not last long. Elijah was in fourth grade at the time. The tensions between his mom and grandma were high. They argued a lot, and on more than one occasion he watched as his mom pulled out a firearm in the middle of a dispute.

Kareem couldn't help noticing the way Elijah reacted

when they ran into his father on the street. The man had always been flamboyant, braggadociously posing with his roll of cash, fat as a grenade. He'd make a scene, peeling off the money note by note. "You need money, Son?"

"Yeah, Daddy."

"Make sure you get whatever you want," he'd say, shooting a quick smile to Kareem as he handed his son $15 or $20. This kind of thing had been happening for as long as Kareem could remember.

By the time Elijah was in fourth grade, he began mirroring a little of his dad's swagger as he walked away, pocketing the money. And while, when he was younger, he had always put up little resistance when his grandmother took the money and used it to buy groceries, he started to say no when he was asked to hand over the cash. "It's mine," he said, his face set in stone. "My daddy gave me this."

Home life became punctuated by arguments, and school life became dominated by Elijah's falling standards. He started smoking and hanging around on the street with the guys who wore red. The Bloods were known to be trouble. The school recommended holding him back in fourth grade, and Kareem worried that Elijah's lack of progress would soon turn into a backslide into the life his mom had failed to escape.

Kareem knew Elijah needed a change—something that was going to harness his natural abilities, plus remove him from the chaos of the neighborhood. He asked whether he might be able to attend Kurn Hattin, a small private boarding school in Vermont. After an initial assessment, the school offered Elijah a slot.

On the first trip to the school, for orientation, Kareem watched as Elijah sat in the hall along with one hundred other students. The teacher up front was talking about politics, and asked whether anyone knew what special event was going to happen the next day. There was silence in the room as blank faces looked away in an effort to avoid getting called on. Only, the silence ended when Elijah's hand shot up and he called out, "Tomorrow's Election Day, sir."

Kurn Hattin turned out to be a great move for Elijah. He stayed in the Friends of the Children program. Kareem maintained his twice-weekly phone calls, and made regular trips up to visit him. Once Elijah became accustomed to good food, getting enough sleep, and the alien luxury of being in the same place night after night (not having to sleep on a couch), his grades started to flourish. All that green space, the cows, the slower pace—all of it was a positive change for him. He learned musical instruments and joined the basketball team, the soccer team, and the baseball team. He became class president, captain of the basketball and baseball teams, and texted Kareem regular updates on his exploits on the court.

I had 35 points and 15 rebounds today. E

That's good. But did you pass the ball at all?

I did but they kept passing it right back to me. Guess they know class when they see it ;) E

Eventually the basketball team made it all the way to the state championship. But it wasn't all smooth sailing for Elijah. The school took the pupils to church every Sunday, and Elijah's naturally inquisitive nature got the better of him one day as he sat in the chapel. Leaning back in his pew, waving for the attention of his teacher, he asked, "Why is there not a black Jesus in here?"

"Not now, Elijah," she replied, trying to let her whisper convey the seriousness of the situation.

"No, I mean it. Why is Jesus always a white guy?"

Repeated attempts to pacify him failed, and pretty soon a full scale argument erupted right there in the church.

When Kareem heard about the incident and Elijah's subsequent suspension, he was annoyed. But he understood Elijah's response as well. Critical thinking was one of the things he had always tried hardest to cultivate in Elijah.

During his years in Vermont, Elijah's thoughts turned toward his mother. Counseling helped him realize that he did not have to end up like his mother, that his future was his own. As he sat in his sessions, Elijah remembered the words Kareem so often spoke to him: "Life's better when you're going toward the pain, not running from it. If you try to escape it, that pain's just going to chase you, and you will never get away. But go toward it, have conversations about the things that bother you, and don't ever be ashamed of your mom's history. In time you'll see it for what it is, and know that you don't have to take that path for yourself."

In early summer, toward the end of eighth grade, Elijah's mom returned home from jail, throwing his whole world into turmoil. "The man you call your dad isn't your real father," she said as they sat in the darkened apartment one afternoon when Elijah was back from school one weekend. "I just said it was him because I didn't want you to know the truth about your real biological father. He raped me. That's how I got pregnant."

Once the shock subsided a little, Elijah had a list of questions that stretched all the way back to Vermont, but the only answers he could get were that the man his mom thought was his real father lived in Atlanta. When she had asked him to take a blood test, he denied every bit of the story. And when the man Elijah had thought of as his father for the first fourteen years of his life heard about all this, he backed off completely. In a matter of weeks, Elijah went from being an enthusiastic, grounded, successful kid on the verge of graduation and enrollment at a prestigious school in upstate New York to a confused, angry young man whose grades flirted with the cliff's edge.

He managed to hold on long enough to graduate Kurn Hattin middle school, but his return to the city for the summer only made matters worse. His former dad wanted nothing to do with him, and home life was punctuated by arguments with his grandma that were more intense than any he had ever experienced. His mom got herself incarcerated again, which only intensified the conflict. Fights could erupt at any time in any place, like the day he and his grandma drove to New Jersey. One little comment was all it took. The fuse was lit. Words were hurled like bombs until she pulled over into a gas station, leaned over, and threw open Elijah's door.

"Get out," she said. "I'm not your mother and I don't have to listen to this. I will not tolerate a disrespectful child." With that, she drove off, leaving Elijah to make his own way back across the Hudson.

At the end of the summer, whether it was from curiosity or from a desire to put the matter to rest—no one was quite sure at first—Elijah's alleged father paid him a surprise visit all the way from Atlanta. They talked, a little nervously at first, but as the minutes slipped by, it became obvious there was a connection. Elijah was instantly drawn to the man. It simply didn't stack up that he had raped his mother.

"I want to go live with him," he said to his grandma after they had all met.

"Oh no, Elijah. This is not going to happen. You're starting a good school and you're on the right track. This is not the time to do this."

Elijah pushed back the only way he knew had a chance of working. He began high school with bad grades that only got worse as the weeks went on. He was determined to be heard, even if meant damaging his future.

Eventually his grandma relented. "Okay," she said. "If you want this to happen, we're going to have to do it the right way. We're going to have to go through the court system. He can legally take responsibility for you. I don't want him to invite you down there and then after six months, say he doesn't want anything to do with you."

Kareem helped Elijah throughout the process, explaining the situation to the school and notifying them when they should cut the financial aid and tuition. He talked a lot with

Elijah about what he felt, what he wanted, and what he hoped would come of it all. Kareem knew Elijah was strong and he knew he was resilient, but was he strong enough? Was he resilient enough?

On the day he was due to get on the bus and take the twenty-hour trip south to begin his new life, Elijah was doing the final packing at his grandma's house. He heard her phone's text alert sound off. After a pause, she appeared in his doorway. Her expression was angry, but broken, too.

Holding out her phone, she said, "I'm sorry."

Elijah read the message.

> *I'm not ready for E to come. Don't put him on the bus.*
> *I'm not in town. I need to rethink the whole situation.*

Elijah put the phone down and looked back at his half-full bags.

Miraculously, there was still space at Kurn Hattin. Kareem was able to convince the school to make the financial aid package available again. What was more remarkable was that Elijah was happy to go back, and that his grades did not follow the usual pattern of tanking when life went wrong like this. He made good progress and kept his grades up. The storms raged in his life, but this time they didn't threaten to sink him.

After four years of studying alongside kids who had two parents, and nice homes, and good manners in church, he had been so excited about the possibility that he too might be able to make a connection with his real father. But having spent fifteen years living face to face with disappointment and trouble, he knew that fantasies like those rarely come true. All he knew for sure was that, whatever lay ahead, he was the only person who was really going to take responsibility for himself.

Throughout the chaos and the changed plans, Elijah had never stopped playing basketball. He had dedicated himself to the sport, knowing that it was his best chance of getting to college. So, still feeling the sting of disappointment from his dad's change of heart, he pushed himself even harder, pushing his body to grow stronger, faster.

Some months after the bus ride that never was, Elijah got a call from his dad. He said that he was sorry about what had happened, and explained that the girl he was living with at the time was not happy about Elijah moving in.

"But we broke up, she's gone now. If you are ready to move down, I am, too."

So Elijah got his wish. He moved down south to live with his dad. Three years later, Elijah began his Senior year at high school. By then he had figured out that Atlanta schools were different from the private establishments of the Northeast, but the change hadn't bothered him as much as he thought it might. After all, he spent too much time on his basketball to really notice whatever else was going on around him. Every day he got up at 6 a.m. and went through his routine: 500 jump shots, weights in the gym, underwater running in the pool. He spent much of the year traveling the country with his AAU basketball club and an even greater amount of time researching which Division 1 College would be the best fit for him. Between the scholarships, the coaches, the facilities, and the current teams, there was a lot to consider.

Life with his dad was going well; even better than he'd expected. His mom was in prison, so it had been a long time since he had seen her, but he managed to get back to Harlem to see the baby sister to whom she had given birth a couple of years earlier. Grandma still kept the apartment darker than a confession booth, and it was strange to watch her with a little child again. She seemed old, but happy. Elijah liked nothing better than to listen to the two of them laughing together.

Now that study and sport had become such increasingly dominant forces in his life, the days when Elijah was in the Friends of the Children program were long gone. But Kareem was still his friend. Both of them knew it would be that way for life.

CHAPTER 17

BREAKING BARRIERS

*"Who could even begin to imagine
the adventures lying ahead?"*

The police said it was an accident. They put it down as a simple case of just another drunk falling over in the park one night, hitting his head on a bench and winding up dead. It was a boilerplate explanation, but it also happened to be wrong. Michelle, the dead man's daughter, knew it couldn't be true. She knew how dangerous the park was at the end of their street. She knew that no death there could ever be accidental, especially not her dad's.

Michelle had almost finished her twelve years in the program, and in that time she had learned how to cope with the things life threw at her better than most. The combination of her father's long term alcoholism, his diabetes, and heart condition, combined with her mother's frequent absences—mysterious trips overseas which could last for weeks at a time—had forced her to take on the role of a caretaker, to find a way of surviving in the middle of the struggle.

Michelle's mom had never been very engaged, and it was one of the things that concerned her kindergarten teachers enough to suggest Michelle as a possible candidate for the program. Also, her older sister had started her own family, which only added to Michelle's sense of rejection.

Then there was the fighting issue.

Michelle was a fighter, a brawler who would take on anyone: peers, older kids, even teachers if she could. She was suspended often, and didn't reserve her outbursts only for school, choosing one day to punch out some glass at the Friends of the Children office. Her hand was badly bruised and needed stitches, but it was clear that the wounds weren't just physical. Her Friend, Kayla, arranged for Michelle to see a counselor in the hope that it would help her express herself in ways that didn't cause so much pain, both to herself and others.

Michelle favored fighting with her fists, but if the anger rose high enough within her then any weapon in easy reach could be brought in to the battle, though she never carried one with her. Most of the people she fought were girls, either from her school or some other nearby place, and her size advantage and complete lack of fear made her a formidable opponent. She enjoyed it, her countenance always failing to suppress the smile that would form whenever she announced, "My friend has beef with some girl; we goin' to fight."

One thing Michelle never did, though, was fight with any girl or boy who was in the program. They were part of her house, her family, and she would never do anything to hurt anyone involved in Friends of the Children. Yet fighting became a way of defining herself. It was a way of being accepted, a way of being known.

Michelle liked having a Friend, even if over the years she lost count of the number of times they said things such as, "there's more to you than fighting" and "how else do you want people to feel about you, apart from fearing you?" With each of the Friends she had over the years, the relationship was solid and dependable. Besides her counselor, her relationship with her Friend was the only one from which she knew she was getting consistent support. That wasn't to say there weren't bumps along the way, and none of her Friends would ever ignore reports of any new fisticuffs in which Michelle had become involved. On those days Michelle would creep in to the office asking, "Is Miss Kayla here? She knows what happened in school today?"

Kayla—like the other Friends—was always there, and she always knew about whatever trouble Michelle had been in that day. Michelle would submit to the earful she knew she was going to get, then the two would put it behind them and get on with it, enjoying the three or four hours they had together. Michelle could have avoided seeing her Friend, she could have disappeared and gone straight home, but a little scolding was always preferable for her to the silence of home.

As the years passed, Michelle's relationship with her mom became increasingly troubled. Often Michelle's mom would promise to take her daughter to exotic destinations and on great days out, but she rarely followed through. Kayla saw the way Michelle would look forward to seeing her mom so much, only to experience intense frustration and sorrow when she realized she'd been let down again. Kayla and her new Friend Jamali learned that it was best for Michelle not to be alone at these times. It didn't take long for them to figure out how to easily share their knowledge with the school and create a plan to help Michelle avoid confrontation at these times.

Eventually Michelle developed a passion for swimming and gymnastics, getting all her energy and anger out of her in a burst during the ninety-minute sessions scheduled for her every Thursday.

When it became a little clearer what her mom was doing when she went away, it helped Michelle to cope: her mom's trips were mainly to Africa, where it was most likely that she was dealing in knock-off designer clothes. More than once she had been caught, even imprisoned there.

By the time Michelle turned eighteen, with her mom in jail in Chad, Michelle was forced to face the death of her dad. With no income, and potentially on the verge of losing her home, Friends of the Children helped Michelle become independent, retaining her dad's social security as well as the apartment. From there she was able to graduate high school, get into a nearby college with a scholarship, and take the first step toward the independent and stable adulthood her parents had never been able to achieve.

At some point during Michelle's program years, someone wondered out loud whether she might have been exposed to violence at home. It was tough to say, though any kid growing up in certain parts of any of the five boroughs would see enough aggression out on the street to make them wonder if fists, knives and guns were simply natural tools for resolving conflict.

Even an innocent Saturday afternoon basketball competition, organized by a few of the Friends, almost turned into a bloodbath one day. Two young men, neither much older than the oldest kids playing, marched toward each other from opposite sides of the basketball courts, weapons drawn. Little children were scooped up in the arms of Friends and everyone ran for the street. It was a miracle nobody was hurt.

Friends need to have certain qualifications on their résumés: a college degree, a couple of years experience working with at-risk children, and the ability to work flexibly within a strong team environment. Yet so much of what makes a good Friend cannot be quantified on paper. They must have enough passion and patience to see them through the inevitable low points that come with the territory. They need the kind of intuition that tells them when to hold the line and when to give a little slack. And without a willing readiness to place themselves in some dangerous social situations, and the wisdom to know how to respond, they'll never take to the work.

After an incident such as the Saturday shooting on the basketball court, it could have been tempting to want to check in with the children and monitor them for any signs that the incident troubled them. Yet while the Friends themselves took a couple of days to process the shock, for some of the children who were present with them, it was just another day in the neighborhood. The kids knew such incidents could happen a few times each week. Children as young as ten or eleven routinely discussed revenge killings or dice games that ended up with weapons drawn and shots fired.

Funerals—whether due to violence or AIDS, diabetes, heart attacks, or substance abuse—are a common occurrence in New York's poorest neighborhoods. One child lost four family members, including his dad and grandfather, between third and fourth grade. While a few have taken up the opportunity to attend a weekend grief camp, most gravitate toward the street, where they remember their loved ones by making custom T-shirts with the faces of their dead on them. They throw block parties in celebration of the life that has passed.

Sadly, a lot of those summer block parties may start out with a DJ, some face painting, a ton of shaved ice, and jump rope competitions, but a lot of them end in violence. All it takes is one game of dice to end badly for one sore loser, and the air can soon enough be filled with gunfire and shouts as people run for safety.

The power of the block is perhaps the hardest thing for outsiders to understand about New York. Despite living less than three minutes walk away from 110th street, it is not uncommon for children to have never visited Central Park. For some people, the block is only to be left when it's absolutely necessary. Even those gang members who make it through adolescence, through their twenties, and out the other side choose to stay on their block. They might have money; they might be at the very top of their food chain. The idea of moving away doesn't appeal to them. Life outside the block is unsafe, dangerous and uncontrollable, so they stay where they feel safe.

The fact that Friends of the Children can reach the children living like this is one of the key things that sets it apart from all other programs. While some potential supporters look at Friends of the Children and wonder whether or not it's an imitation of Big Brothers Big Sisters, the truth is that Friends of the Children reaches those kids who would never end up with either a Big Brother or a Big Sister. The parents and guardians with whom Friends of the Children work wouldn't know about the opportunity to nominate their child for a Friend, much less would they know how to fill out the required paperwork and attend a meeting. Yet these parents and guardians of the children, trapped as they so often are in a cycle of poverty, drug addiction and criminal activity, are often the program's loudest cheerleaders.

Gradually, the word about Friends of the Children has started to spread through the city and across the country. In 2012 it was named by the Social Impact Exchange as one of the top hundred charities in the country. In 2015, it was named the most admired nonprofit in Oregon. Articles in *The New York Times, Fortune,* and *Forbes* introduced Friends of the Children to new supporters and charitable foundations. Most were drawn to the fact that the program could prove that it had the impact it said it had.

Another factor that has always helped Friends of the Children to stand out is that they start early in a child's life and work with them long-term. Nobody but Friends of the Children keeps kids for twelve years, and nobody else is as intentional with the most at-risk kids in society from such an early age. Consequently, this means there are no competitors, which makes it difficult to compare the program against other nonprofits. Almost inevitably in a discussion that introduces

Friends of the Children, Big Brother Big Sister will come up, and some people are surprised to hear that while Big Brother Big Sister spends $1,300[4] a year per child, the costs for Friends of the Children to work with a child for a year are closer to $10,000. Yet Friends of the Children reaches places and people Big Brothers and Big Sisters cannot. Friends routinely walk past drug deals in hallways, they walk into apartments filled with the unmistakable smell of pot. Helping the most at-risk kids in a society demands a special kind of person. Changing the lives of children who otherwise would end up dropping out of school, pregnant, incarcerated or dead is a full time job.

For that, Friends of the Children requires long-term commitment, about which they talk openly with potential funders. "It sounds like you expect us to stay with you forever," one of them said while taking a tour of the offices.

"That's right," came the reply. "Just like our kids, we're here for the long haul."

That same long-term commitment is in evidence from the Friends as well. While Friends of the Children asks for at least a three-year commitment for employment, of those who qualify and are offered a job, the average tenure is over seven years.

Around the time the children in the first class of Friends of the Children program graduated, the lease on the program's original office expired. The increased pace of

---

[4]Blueprints for Healthy Youth Development, Big Brothers Big Sisters of America Program Rating; http://www.blueprintsprograms.com/program-Costs.php?pid=fe5dbbcea5ce7e2988b8c69bcfdfde8904aabc1f

gentrification made it hard work to find a suitable property, but eventually something turned up. The only problem was that it needed $100,000 to fund it.

Bob Houck, the Friends of the Children New York's Executive Director, was on the phone with someone from one of the foundations that had been supporting the program the longest. Bob mentioned the building in passing, explaining that it looked as though they were probably going to have to forget about it because they simply didn't have the funds. "I'm sorry to hear that," said his contact at the Pinkerton Foundation, after which he wished Bob well and said good-bye.

A few minutes later, Bob's phone rang. It was the Pinkerton Foundation. "Okay," said the familiar voice. "We just had a meeting, and we're going to give you $100,000. Go get that office."

Part of the irony of life for those growing up in the five boroughs is that even though they live so close to opportunity in New York, there is an invisible barrier keeping them from it. Yet with a Friend at their side, the children visit museums and play mini-golf. They feed ducks and ride subways, go fishing and visit the Apollo Theater. They go rock climbing and bike riding. They learn about art and explore the world through a thousand different eyes. And eventually something will spark, a passion will be ignited, and the long process of finding something to live, dream, and work for will leap into motion.

It can be a delicate process. When a child who has never traveled farther than three or four blocks from his or her home gets a load of the perks available in a globally major city, the experience can be overwhelming. So the Friends take it slow, going downtown one week, visiting a local park the next. With every outing, the Friend helps guide the child toward certain goals, anything from word recognition to people skills, from telling time to personal safety.

This was how it was for Imani. She was six when she joined the program. Her teen mother had recently left the city and moved to North Carolina for work, leaving Imani with her grandparents. It was a painful experience for her, and the rejection threatened to undermine the foundation of her life. And yet it was not the beginning of the end. It was the start of something new.

Through countless activities and day trips, a succession of Friends guided Imani. They showed her people achieving great things, adults who had grown up on the same streets. The talked about powerful women and the strength that comes from within. They helped to open her eyes and stimulate her appetite, but it was Imani—with the support of her grandparents—who set her course. Friends of the Children showed her the view. Imani was the one who stepped into the adventure.

As the years passed, Imani discovered new talents and strengths. She excelled academically, winning a spot in the Future Leaders Institute Charter School, an academically rigorous, extended-year program in Harlem. She became an even more avid reader, devouring mysteries with an insatiable appetite. By the time she was fifteen, Imani had earned a scholarship to a competitive Manhattan high school. Soon after that, her Friend took her out to a running track. She was a natural, and became a talented sprinter. Later still, she won a spot on the school's cheerleading squad.

There was no stopping her. Ten years after she was abandoned by her mom, she walked out onto the stage at the Apollo Theater. It was amateur night, but as ever, there was nothing second-rate or clunky about the performances. The crowd expected every performer to excel, to be worthy of stepping onto the same stage on which Ella Fitzgerald and Billie Holiday had made their debuts. On that night, Imani made her own debut, bringing the crowd to their feet and filling the air with shouts and cheers. She clinched second place.

If you believe the statistics, Imani should have followed in the footsteps of her teenage mother. She should have dropped out of high school and lived the rest of her life bouncing from one crisis to another. Yet Imani chose to forge another story. Even before her childhood was over, she had achieved far more than many adults ever do. Who could even begin to imagine the adventures that lay ahead?

CHAPTER 18

TRAINING FOR A MARATHON, NOT A SPRINT

*"I've heard a lot about you.
I'm glad you're in my son's life."*

N ot every new Friends of the Children venture that started fared that well. The chapter founded in Cincinnati in 2002 closed down by the time the decade closed out. It was the first time a chapter had been started with public rather than private money, and when the economy crashed in 2008, the chapter's public funding dried up.

Having spent a lifetime exemplifying that Campbells don't quit, Duncan was devastated to discover that neither he nor the team that ran the newly established national office for Friends of the Children were able to do anything to help Cincinnati remain open.

For Duncan, the businessman who for years had listened to people tell him no and stared down failure more times than he could remember, the close of the Cincinnati chapter was a bitter pill to swallow. But it wasn't a fatal blow. He and the team learned some important lessons from the failed chapter. They learned how vital it is to encourage financial resiliency in them, how to work best with the kind of social innovators and investors that are naturally drawn to similar programs, and how to keep good lines of communication open between the different chapters around the country.

But New York was different. In the time it took for Elijah, Michelle, and Jazmin to enter and finally graduate the program, Friends of the Children New York managed to find its footing and grow. But not only grow—it had begun to thrive. In its infancy the program struggled to be recognized as a serious force for good in the community. It took years before people appreciated the effectiveness of the unique mentoring project. During that time, most conversations about talented organizations doing great work in Upper Manhattan focused on the Harlem Children's Zone, a nonprofit organization working among poverty-stricken children and families.

Harlem Children's Zone's parenting workshops, its preschool program, its public charter schools and its health programs—plus the two episodes of *60 Minutes* and a few interviews on *Charlie Rose*—routinely eclipsed Friends of the Children New York when it came to fundraising and name recognition. But in its dedication to "doing nothing less than breaking the cycle of generational poverty for the thousands of children and families it serves," it was easy to see that the same DNA existed in the vision that had first captivated Duncan and Orin. In time the two organizations became partners, united by a common desire to transform lives.

Some of the children who were helped by Harlem Children's Zone were also part of the Friends of the Children program. In such situations, the work of both nonprofits added value to the other. Harlem Children's Zone supported the family, while Friends of the Children focused on the child. If it takes a village to raise a child, then why shouldn't it take an army of dedicated community workers to help an entire family? Children and their families living in a community full of obstacles to enjoying a safe and prosperous life need all the help they can get—not only for their own wellbeing but also for the well-being of the community.

For Kareem, Kayla, and the other Friends—just as it has been for those working at all the other chapters—it has been vital for the program to adapt to meet the changing needs of the children. When those involved in the New York chapter realized that their teenage children were missing appointments and drifting away, Friends New York changed its structure, introducing the adolescent program already underway in Portland. Within six months after the Friends started to spend time with their children all together as a group rather than one on one, they saw a 30 percent drop in cancelled appointments.

Friends of the Children New York introduced an intern program, empowering fifteen- and sixteen-year-old children valuable experience working with companies throughout the city. In the process they helped the children fill out their resumes, sit through practice interviews and—for one day each week—learn how to manage their checkbook, how to dress properly for interviews and the workplace, and many other things that other kids absorb from their parents.

Yet as far as Friends of the Children New York has come, everyone involved is aware of the distance it has yet to travel. Having established the work in Harlem, they pushed northward to South Bronx, opening a satellite office just outside Hunts Point in 2014.

Even though the drive to South Bronx from the office in Harlem was less than twenty minutes, their differences were clear from the start: A bigger Hispanic population meant there were larger, stronger family units. The heavier drug use meant even more unpredictability and danger on the streets. There was a little less gang activity in South Bronx than Harlem, but there was more poverty. In fact, in the entire nation there were few districts experiencing greater poverty than South Bronx.

From 2007 to 2014, Friends of the Children New York grew from serving sixty children on a budget of $500,000 to serving 160 children on a budget of $2 million. Much like Portland—before the work began expanding nationally—it was important that the burgeoning branch in South Bronx develop its own structure and staff. This foundation was vital for the New York Friends program to continue to run smoothly. In the same way that Duncan looked out across the country and saw the need for more chapters in more cities, so Bob Houck, Kareem, and the rest of the team in New York were acutely aware of the need for Friends to find a way to work with children in Brooklyn, Queens and Staten Island.

To do that, they will need more people like Richard. A former banker and long time Harlem resident, Richard walked everywhere. His height caused him to be a memorable character in the community. After all, he wasn't just tall, he was basketball tall. But it was his dedication to working with youth that has made the biggest impression on Harlem. Parents trusted and respected him. Children wanted to learn from him. And one humid Saturday afternoon when two gunmen converged on the basketball court, it was Richard who stood his ground and ensured everyone escaped safely.

Richard was one of the first Friends in New York and Carl was one of the first kids he met. Carl was eight years old at the time, squeaking his way around the basketball court in the school gym. As someone who played the center position in college, Richard watched from the side of the court. Richard remembered how, when he was eight years old, his biggest challenge was learning how to dribble the ball. Carl was a different story. It was clear that he was a long way beyond the basic skill stage, and his ball handling and shooting—his whole skill set—was exceptional. *That kid's doing things that no eight-year-old should be able to do,* Richard thought. *He's got skills.*

Richard became Carl's Friend. Basketball became their connection. Richard lost count of the number of times he heard a teacher tell Carl to "sit still and concentrate," and it was only through sport that some of that energy could begin to be channeled. The boy had been diagnosed with ADHD and, on paper at least, had all the makings of a kid who was likely to end up in the Juvenile Justice System.

Having grown up in Queens and lived his adult life in Harlem, Richard understood the reality of Carl's life. He knew that having a father who was incarcerated was tough, and with school not being the most enjoyable place, it meant Carl remained at high risk to slip into gang activity. So, like so many Friends with their children, Richard set about introducing Carl to a world beyond the block.

Even though his home was on 127th, Carl had never been to the Apollo Theater, only two blocks away, on 125th, or to the Central Park Conservatory Garden.

One day Richard took him north to visit a museum—and Carl couldn't believe it.

"You're crazy, Mr. Richard," he said. "There's no museum in Harlem."

But within an hour they were both standing, open-mouthed, in front of the medieval art on display at The Cloisters at the Met.

For many children, such trips provide a spark that ignites an unrealized passion inside them to work hard, and for their *chosen* future. For Carl—who already knew precisely how he wanted his life to play out—hanging out with Richard provided him with something that was all too often missing from his day-to-day life: a father figure who would commit the time and the energy to be with him.

One day when he went to visit Carl, Richard paused before he rang the buzzer of his child's apartment. He felt something he had never experienced at any other time when visiting Carl: he felt nervous. For the first two years Richard and Carl had worked together, Carl's father, Jerry, was incarcerated. But he had been recently released, and it was time for the two men to meet.

Richard wondered what it was going to mean. Would Carl's

dad see him as an impostor? Would he feel threatened? Would he resent the close bond that had formed between the man he had never met and the son from whom he had been so absent? And if any of the above were true, how would he react? Would he be hostile? Might things even become violent?

Carl opened the door, and Richard walked in. He knew the apartment well, but he noticed of himself that he was hanging back a little more than usual, waiting for Carl to take the lead and head back to the kitchen. As he did, Richard saw Jerry for the first time. Jerry was seated at a small table that had been pressed up against the wall. He looked to be about the same age as Richard. His hair was braided, and his hands were clasped together in front of him on the table. He stared at Richard. Nothing about him suggested warmth or friendship. Every part of him communicated menace.

"This is my dad," Carl said.

Introductions didn't go much further.

Carl's dad pushed back his chair, standing up. "So you're Mr. Richard," Jerry said. "I've heard a lot about you." There was a pause. Then he said, "I'm glad you're in my son's life."

The two men shook hands.

Richard exhaled. "It's good to meet you too, sir."

The two men talked awhile, though in the end Richard would barely remember about what. Mostly he was relieved and surprised by Jerry's positive reaction.

"Anyway," Jerry said, "You two gotta go. Take Carl out and have some fun."

Outside, it struck Richard that he was taking Carl away from his dad, a man who was clearly much nicer than what he'd feared. "Are you sure you want to come out with me today? It's fine if you'd rather stay home with your dad."

"I know he's home," Carl said, "but I planned to hang out with you."

They left it at that, heading for the park.

It was obvious there were worse fathers in the neighborhood than Carl's. When it came to providing for his family, Jerry was good enough. He worked construction in the summer, bringing home his earnings. But when he was home, he did nothing but watch TV and hang around the house. Even though their block, on 127th, was pretty safe—the tougher blocks were a couple of streets away—Carl's dad seemed to want to lock himself away from the rest of the world, if only to keep Carl away from getting recruited by a local gang.

Gangs, like predators, single out the weak. They know who doesn't have a father around, they know who needs a family. "Join us," they say, "and we'll take care of you. We'll give you money and protection. All the things you're missing." And once a kid joins a gang, the acceptance and support they get from it can be intoxicating. For someone who has been denied a loving family, being part of a gang can tap into their primal need for safety and community. Add to that the fact that they can make thousands of dollars in a single day, and the appeal is obvious. Why else would someone join an organization in which 90 percent of its members are arrested by the time they turn eighteen, 95 percent don't finish high school, and 60 percent are dead or in prison by the time they hit twenty? For gang members in America, the average life expectancy is twenty years and five months. Gangs offer a desperate way of life to those whose life is desperately out of options.[5]

While Carl had a handful of friends who had been heavily recruited into gangs, the few attempts that members of the Bloods had made to try to bring him in had been halfhearted and short-lived.

For one thing, Carl was busy with sports and his outings with Richard. He didn't have the time to become bored or hang around on the street and get into trouble. But the main factor keeping him out of gang activity was the gangs themselves. From an early age Carl had obvious potential that everyone could see. His skill on the basketball court was so great that he, more than anyone else from his neighborhood, had a real chance of going somewhere.

The message about Carl was clear: hands off.

Even the gang members didn't want to mess with that kind of hope.

One day Richard told Carl he had extra tickets to a track and field event at Madison Square Garden. "Do you think your dad would want to join us?" he asked.

Carl said it was likely.

And when they asked Jerry, he said, "Sure."

The three of them, one exceptionally tall, another looking hard and tired, and the boy jumping along between them, got on the subway heading south. It was an odd-looking trio, but there was nothing odd about the way the three bonded.

Over the coming months, the three spent more time

---

[5] http://police.conroeisd.net/docs/mastergang.pdf

together on outings. When Carl had a basketball or football game Jerry would be there, comparing notes with Richard from the stands about how his son was progressing.

"You know," Jerry said to Richard late one afternoon as they walked away from the court together, "I'm glad that I got to see what you do with my son. You're making me a better father. Now I know what I need to do with him as his father. I need to step up."

Richard didn't know quite what to say.

Through the years that he was Carl's Friend, Richard prioritized the importance of consistency in Carl's life. Whenever his father went to jail, Carl's schoolwork would falter. This was hardly a surprise, so Richard tried to encourage Carl to talk about it. This was a conversation to which they returned many times over the years.

Like jigsaw pieces laid down in order, the full picture of how Carl felt finally emerged. "We had a good time together when he was out, but what was it all for if he's just going to go away again? When he goes it hurts me. We just got close this time. I want to make him proud, but why should I bother? He's not here to see it."

It took five or six years before Richard could have a conversation about jail with Jerry. "I was in jail for drugs," he said. "When there's no construction work in the winter, I have nothing to do, and no other way of making money, so I sell drugs. Mr. Richard, I have to take care of my family, and this is the only way I know how."

Richard thought for a while, wondering if he would be allowed to say what he wanted to say. "But you get caught.

You get sent to jail." He took a breath and said, "You're not very good at it."

"I know. I need to stop."

"So why not stop? Don't you think Carl would rather be hungry and have you around than be able to have a new pair of kicks and lose you for two years?"

Jerry agreed that he would try to do better. And he did for a while.

Carl graduated high school with an impressive resume. Having grown to love football as much as basketball, he made a late switch, becoming ranked as one of the top two quarterbacks in the state. He held records for the most completions, most touchdowns, and highest total yardage.

In spite of his dad getting incarcerated again during his sophomore year, Carl started making good choices, like who to take to the prom.

Carl and Michelle had both been in the program since kindergarten. They were close friends, and it bothered him that she didn't have a date for the prom. He told her, "You're not going to prom by yourself. I'm going with you. I'm going to be your prom date."

Michelle was thrilled.

Richard was taken aback, though pleased.

"Really?" said Richard when he heard about it. Carl was the kind of boy who could take any girl he wanted to take to prom. Michelle was tough and hardened, the kind of girl who most boys tried to avoid, afraid she might beat them up if they got into an argument.

"Yes, Mr. Richard. Michelle's not going alone." And Carl

made good on his promise.

Carl continued to make good choices past high school. His dad's absence during his sophomore year had produced a crash in his grades, and the damage to his academic record ruled him out of consideration for Division I schools. But Carl refused to let that throw him off course. He enrolled in a community college, made it on to the team as the third-string quarterback and red-shirted for the first football season because he wasn't getting enough playing time. He attended every practice, dressed for each game, and turned his mind away from whatever short-term frustration he felt at the time. He was playing the long game. He remembered what Richard always said to him: "You're going somewhere. Don't let what's happened to you in the past change any of that."

In the world of competitive distance running, the concept of the negative split plays a vital role. It is a simple enough idea. Runners deliberately tackle the first half of the race slower than the second, giving themselves time to find a pace and improve on it. The negative split allows runners to keep enough in the tank to thunder across those final miles, picking off weaker, less disciplined competitors who tire too early.

Though they don't know it during childhood, kids like Carl, Michelle, and Elijah—as well as Little Ninja, Ben, Nicky, and all the others—were being trained to tackle life like seasoned marathon runners.

They learned discipline; the long game. They learned to fight the urge to panic and trust the wisdom they'd gained through their own hard work and hard-won experiences. They learned not to yield to the pressure, but instead to run their own race. They learned about ambition and application, about the sweet feeling that accompanies a well-earned reward.

As they learned to live out the negative split, they discovered that they too can be serious about going the distance, fulfilling—even stretching—their potential.

But they weren't the only ones doing it. Friends of the Children embraces a constantly evolving, ever-learning, never-resting appetite for improving at what it does. With every passing year, the program strives to reduce the numbers of children who are at-risk in America by equipping them to succeed in whatever ventures they pursue.

The negative split is bound to have increasingly positive results.

PART FOUR

HOPE
FOR
THE FUTURE

CHAPTER 19

WITNESSING THE POWER
OF TRUE TRANSFORMATION

"Mark has become part of the family."

D ressed in a suit and looking around the elegantly decorated conference room, Duncan was tempted to wish he was wearing hiking boots and staring out across a sea of Pacific Northwest timber. But he knew he was in the right place, that it was good to be surrounded by so many other people, with their nice clothes and easy conversation.

It was 2009, and Duncan had been nominated for the Purpose Prize, an annual award for social innovators over fifty years old who work creatively to spearhead significant change. Just to be one of the 1,000 people nominated is an acknowledgment that you're making a significant impact on important social issues, with the potential to have even greater impact in the future. To be one of the ten winners—and get sent home with prizes of $50,000 to $100,000 to support your work—is something else entirely. Duncan was one of them.

Duncan Campbell, a throwaway kid from Portland who overcame the odds, heard his name called. He walked carefully up to the podium. After a quick handshake and a look at the heavy glass prize that had been handed to him, he turned to the microphone. "The last fifteen years of my life have given me more meaning, satisfaction, and contentment than I ever could have imagined. This," he said, "is the best part of my life.

"I'm humbled to win this prize, just as I'm humbled whenever I'm stopped on the street by strangers who tell me that their child or grandchild is in the Friends of the Children program, and finally has hope for the future. I'm humbled today the same as I am when I get letters like the one I received from a high school freshman who has been in the Friends program for twelve years. She reminded me that she was abandoned by her father and mother, going to live with an aunt who routinely abused her. She wrote how her Friend gave her so much: For the first time someone cared about her, believed she had value, and validated her thoughts and feelings. Her Friend, she wrote, has changed everything."

In 2010, Duncan left his business Campbell Global and turned to his deepest love: Friends of the Children. After seventeen years of experience and thousands of children across the United States being helped by a Friend, he had a clear goal in mind: to grow the program toward a goal of working in twenty cities within the next twenty years. New York was successfully established and new chapters had taken root elsewhere; one in Boston and another in Seattle, where a former Microsoft executive had invested more than

THE ART OF BEING THERE| 233

$1 million of his own money to get the project started.

All the knowledge and all the experience that Duncan had gained over the years was valuable, but for Friends of the Children to scale up and begin making a significant impact on the children of the country, he needed to communicate to a far wider range of people about the value of their work. Part of the challenge Friends of the Children faced was honing its message to various supporters and other foundations who were more narrow in their scope. Friends of the Children prevents so many things: dropping out of high school, early pregnancies, a glut of kids in the nation's juvenile justice system. Many traditional funding streams prefer to focus on specific problems, tackling single issues rather than complex webs of problems. But poverty and risk are neither neat nor simple problems.

Press coverage and a slick website wasn't all Duncan needed. There was the matter of money, and lots of it. In the early years he'd been able to fund the program himself, and even once it had grown, it was still possible to raise the funds required from a relatively small number of private donors and trusts. But to make the impact Duncan and his staff believed they could make, they needed the kind of funding that only came from the public purse. And to get that they would have to prove beyond all doubt that Friends of the Children really was capable of making the kind of impact he had always said it was. He needed hard evidence: a formal random cohort research study. If it helped Friends of the Children reach their goal, he was ready to lend his support to a full-scale clinical trial.

234 | DUNCAN CAMPBELL

While Duncan was considering this, that year members of the Harvard Business School Association of Oregon approached Friends of the Children, asking whether they could carry out an intense study of the Portland chapter. They quantified the economic benefits to society by comparing young people in the Friends program to a population of Portland-area kids with the same background—race, income, and education—who had no Friend.

Those who graduated from Friends of the Children earned high school diplomas, avoided juvenile justice, and were far better at avoiding teen pregnancy than kids who had no Friend. And while the results were encouraging, what really made the difference was the fact that the study pegged these positive outcomes to dollar amounts saved in the community.

A kid with a high school degree will get a better paying job than someone who drops out. They'll end up paying more taxes and using fewer government services—welfare, food stamps and Section 8 housing. If Friends of the Children kept kids out of prison, the state wouldn't need to hire more guards and build more institutions. A girl who doesn't have a baby as a minor will place less of a strain on social services. And all of those differences affect taxpayers' pocketbooks. Friends of the Children's work was never truly about dollar amounts—it was about transforming people's lives and breaking generational cycles of poverty. But quantifying their work seemed to open outsiders' eyes beyond the powerful anecdotes.

By calculating the costs, researchers were able to put a

dollar value on Portland's Friends of the Children chapter. The return on investment was staggering: for every $1 spent on Friends of the Children, society received nearly $7 in benefits.

If it were an investment in the stock market, it would be heralded as one deal that would be difficult to turn down. There had never been any doubt that the program worked, but to see the extent of its impact so clearly mapped was nothing short of astounding.

The Harvard study spurred the team on, paving the way toward a longer-term national study. Launched with funding provided by a division of the National Institutes of Health, researchers at the University of Washington and Princeton University are, as of this writing, managing an intensive "longitudinal randomized control trial study" of Friends of the Children called The Child Study.

Though it won't be complete for some time, The Child Study is the gold standard, a rigorous evaluation of Friends of the Children chapters in Portland, Seattle, New York City, and Boston. As many as twenty researchers are involved, all taking a hard look at each chapter in a random control trial to evaluate the program.

Of the 278 children in the trial, half have a Friend and half do not. Every year, researchers interview the children— those with and without a Friend—as well as their parents and guardians, along with the Friends. They also interview teachers and pull school records to chart what's happening in the children's lives.

If the study shows what Duncan has already witnessed, it

will affirm that Friends of the Children is one of the most effective programs developed to bring about transformative change while breaking the cycle of poverty in people's lives. While every nonprofit has passionate people and many organizations claim they're having positive impacts, in the world of funding, people don't take things at face value. Those in charge of well-funded philanthropies want to see proven results especially when you're asking for the amount of money that Friends of the Children will need to expand into metropolitan cities and communities all across the country and beyond.

Thanks to the sleeper effect, which describes the time lag that it takes for the first shoots of change to emerge from a relationship like that between a Friend and their child, the most significant findings will occur when the children are older—when they become teenagers and begin making choices about whether to drop out of school or engage in risky, even criminal, behavior. Meanwhile, there are no shortage of cheerleaders and local evaluators shouting about the Friends of the Children's model success.

Rarely will a week go by without Duncan reminding Friends of the Children staff about their objective. "Our aim is to eradicate childhood poverty," he says. He likes to pause a little at that point to let the words sink in, knowing precisely how audacious a claim it is. Then he likes to follow up with another one: "We found the solution to the end of generational poverty." Pause. "We broke the cycle. We worked out a way of helping these people who fill our prisons, who fail academically in our schools and who bring new children into their world of chaos. We've got the solution that can help them become productive members of society."

He's not alone. There are plenty of others lining up to add their voice to the chorus of support for Friends of the Children. Teachers, parents, Friends; they all have a tale to tell, like John, for example.

As a public school teacher who has had several students enrolled in the Friends of the Children program, John holds a unique perspective about the program—a perspective that needs to be heard. "Most people never see these kids," John says. "That makes it easy for them not to know anything about the world they live in and the struggles they encounter day after day. But these are the kids that slip through the cracks."

These are the students that are being lost. Every day that they come to school they bring a whole range of issues with them: the complexities and struggles that come from living in a foster home, the slow agony of poverty, the hollow feeling that comes from having an incarcerated parent, the shame and fear of abuse. They bring all these things to class, sometimes acting out because of them, sometimes trying desperately to hold all those painful emotions in. They can be aggressive, angry, awkward, argumentative, and plenty of other adjectives that would work all the way through the alphabet to the letter Z. But John, like so many other teachers who work among America's most at-risk children, knows that the one thing that all of them need is a lot of love.

"It wasn't until my second year of teaching that I heard about Friends of the Children. What more could a teacher

238 | DUNCAN CAMPBELL

ask for than a person who was dedicated to helping the most troubled and troublesome kid in his class?

"By second grade, many of my students have moved as many as five times, which often means that their schooling falls off a cliff. Last year I had a student in the program who had been with a foster family for two years when he was adopted. Instead of saying goodbye and wishing him well for the future, the transition was harsh, cold, and heartless: the foster family simply brought his stuff to the school office and said they were done with him. He already had issues with trust, and when the adoptive family said they didn't want him to finish the year in my classroom, it looked to me like it was going to make things a whole lot worse.

"I felt powerless, aware that my role stopped at the classroom door. The only positive thing was that this child had a Friend. He was the one constant in this student's life. He helped the child through the transition, navigating the pain and fear that accompanied every stage, making sure that he got acclimated to his new school and made the best start possible. His Friend brought him back in the spring to visit the classroom and in the summer I met his adoptive parents when I was invited to the boy's birthday party. I witnessed the changes in this boy's life. He was going to be just fine. None of this would have happened without Friends of the Children."

It's slow work, but like many teachers, John has seen the impact that a Friend can make on a child in real time. So many of the kids have heard nothing but abuse, disdain, mockery or open hostility. Bit by bit, outing by outing, conversation by conversation, he has seen the change in children as they start to hear new messages about themselves: that they can succeed, they can achieve, they can make choices. Bit by bit, he has watched as they start to grow.

For parents, the idea of accepting the offer of a place in the program for their child can be complicated. Can they trust a stranger with their child? Does their child even need this kind of intervention? What does it say about their home life?

"I got a call from the teacher telling me that my son had been picked," Mallory said, "and I thought *how can my son be troubled in kindergarten?* He was a good boy. But the more I thought about it, I realized there might be issues."

Her son's father was not a part of his life. Instead, he was in and out of jail. Life as a single parent was tough on both of them. Mallory worked late shifts as a bar manager while her son attended three schools before he finished kindergarten. Each day Mallory would wake up, see her son for an hour in the morning before he went to the sitter and then to school. When she got home, he'd always be asleep.

"I was a little suspicious about Friends of the Children. I spent two weeks thinking about it. I talked with people I trusted. My mom was worried. She wondered who this Friend would be and told me to be careful and to watch out. But it was when my son and I went to an open house for all the kids who had been selected that I started to feel good about it. I found out they did a background check on the Friends, and while we were there, my son played with other kids. On the way home, he told me that he wanted to be a part of the program."

The next step was for Mallory and her son to meet the

Friend, Mark. "I was fine talking with Mark on the telephone, but I felt so nervous when he showed up at my door. How do you build trust with a stranger? We just talked, and I learned about Mark and his life. He made me feel at ease."

Two years later, Mallory can already see the ways in which life is better for her son. "Mark has taken him to so many new places, and he's done so many new things. He got my son into a breakdancing class, which amazed me because my son used to always say, 'I can't do that.' But Mark took him to the classes, he encouraged him. My son learned, he did it. And what's more important than the dancing is the fact that my son got the 'I can't' out of his vocabulary. He tries hard now. He believes in himself and in what he can do in all areas of his life."

Mark has become part of the family. He talks with Mallory about her life and his, about her son and about the way he's growing up. They talk about the successes and the challenges and about how it's good that her son finally has someone other than his mother on whom he can rely and confide in.

"What's amazing," Mallory said, "is that this person who was once a stranger is now present in my child's life, changing his life for the better."

For the Friends themselves, the job is unique. They are not social workers, parents, teachers or counselors, yet being a Friend requires all the skills normally expected of a candidate for any of those posts. They must have empathy and an understanding of what life is like for the kids they work with, but they must also be able to show the kids a wider world, helping each discover—and begin to fulfill—their potential.

Those Friends who come from the same kind of communities in which they serve know what is required in order to break out of poverty: the resilience and the support of good people who care enough to cheer them on. So it's hardly surprising that many of the Friends have their own unique stories to tell, stories like Nicky's: the girl who climbed to the thin branches dreaming of escape from the toxic words of home, but who found that rescue was closer at hand than she dared to believe.

"I remember what it felt like to watch my mom and my aunt drink their way through life. I'd be counting down the moments until the violence erupted, part of me wanting to freeze and become invisible, another part telling me that I needed to run out of there fast. Only once I got to the park and climbed up high in the cedar trees did I relax. And that's when I wished I was old.

"That was twenty years ago. I've aged past the age I used to wish to be when I was up in the branches. A lot has happened in that time; meeting Matt, getting into the program myself, my grandma passing, me finally standing up to my aunt, Matt giving up his job to care for us, me graduating high school, and me making it to college. In so many ways, life has worked out even better than I hoped it would. I was able to cope with the transition to college, I made new friends and got a job—first as an Outward Bound counselor, then in the college admissions department. I graduated. I experienced the biggest eureka moment of my life: Now that I have earned my college degree, my aunt can't say I won't amount to anything.

"But there's one thing about leaving my childhood behind that was really hard: it was Matt telling me he had been diagnosed with cancer. He fought hard. It didn't stop us from spending time together. He saw me graduate, and we talked a lot about what I would do next. He listened as I told him about how I wanted to be a high school history teacher in inner city areas. I listened as he talked about how much he loved his job as a Friend. It was a huge struggle to watch him get sicker and sicker, but I never lost the feeling that we were blessed to have had him in our lives.

"In 2011—the year I got married—Matt passed away. I was working at the Y as a site director for an elementary school, getting a sense of what it might be like to go into teaching. I liked it, but I knew that I could do more.

"I knew I wanted to be a Friend.

"I called Friends of the Children and asked if they were hiring. They were. There was a vacancy to start that winter, but I wanted to finish out the school year with my kids. They told me I could wait, and apply when they would be hiring again in the spring. So I waited, working on my cover letter and resume, getting each of my old Friends to write letters of recommendation. I didn't know if they would hire me, but I had all these qualifications and all this experience. I thought I should be fine, but I didn't know for sure.

"When I heard I got the job, I phoned Matt's parents. I told them I don't think I'd be where I am now if I hadn't met Matt."

In 2012, Nicky became the first graduate of the Friends

program to be employed by Friends of the Children. Like Matt, and the many others who have gone before her, she has dedicated herself to helping each of the eight girls that have been placed with her. Like Duncan, Kareem, and dozens of others, she'll walk with them side by side, taking small steps. Through countless conversations and experiences, Nicky glides away from a life of risk and danger and out toward a fuller, safer, longer life.

***

THERE ARE 2.2 MILLION CHILDREN in the United States who are under six years old and living in extreme poverty[6]. That's approximately the same population as countries like Latvia or Namibia. It's the same number of people who live in Houston, Texas. And it's the same size as the U.S. current prison population.

It can be hard to imagine what life is like for those 2.2 million, and so much of modern day life dissuades others from having any meaningful contact with them. With a problem this big, perhaps it seems so overwhelming and hopeless.

But as a society, we cannot ignore these children.

People who want to help bring about transformative change cannot subscribe to the myth that if these children fail at the one or two chances society gives them it means they

[6] National Center for Child Poverty,
http://www.nccp.org/tools/risk/?state=OR&age-level=6&income-level=Poor&ids[]=76&ids[]=72&ids[]=83&submit=Recalculate

simply didn't want change bad enough. We cannot assume that their acceptance of disappointment is a sign that they should be left alone to fend for themselves. We cannot console ourselves with the notion that the cycle of generational poverty is too hard to break.

Unless something dramatic happens, we know what will happen to those 2.2 million children who live within our borders, children who are enrolled in our schools and share our streets. They are the ones most likely to become the next wave of teen parents, the next class of high school dropouts, the next generation of children caught up in the Juvenile Justice System. Unless something changes, most of those 2.2 million children who grow up in poverty will pass that same poverty and those same bleak prospects on to their children, creating a new generation of at-risk children born into an at-risk world.

In the years Friends of the Children has spent working among these children, a clear picture of some of the lives that make up these 2.2 million has emerged. Like an image slowly pulling into focus, the truth has been revealed. Every one of the 400,000[7] children in the foster care system is a part of that crowd of 2.2 million.

As Friends' National President Terri Sorensen says, "The broken public systems want to serve kids short term, while they're in an abusive situation, while they're on food stamps or in some other trouble. You can keep on throwing $70,000

[7] KidsCount DataCenter, 2013 Report
http://datacenter.kidscount.org/data/Tables/6243-children-in-foster-care?loc=1&loct=1#detailed/1/any/false/36,868,867,133,38/any/12987

per year at an incarcerated juvenile, or you can step in earlier and prevent the problem from the start. That's where we're concentrating all our efforts. And that's why what we're doing works."

All of the children who have been removed from their homes by the state are classified as at-risk children by the government. While the foster care system works to offer safety to those children, some in its care can expect to be moved between nine and twelve times throughout their childhood. With that kind of uncertainty and turbulence, it's not surprising many are starting to ask how the foster care system can do better investing in wellbeing.

A clear challenge has come from these children and from the leaders who champion their cause. Friends of the Children has something unique to offer those in the foster care system, and while outcomes for unsupported children within the foster care system are grim, long-term outcomes for those foster children who are enrolled with Friends of the Children are almost as good as they are for those in the program who still live with their biological family. Though 5 percent fewer avoid the Juvenile Justice System (88 percent as opposed to 93 percent) the same percentage gain their GED, graduate high school and avoid teen parenting.[8] With a Friend dedicated to their well-being from age five through nineteen, all that uncertainty and turbulence slowly begins to loosen its grip.

---

[8] Kissick, K. Mackin J.R. & Redfield, M. (2016). *Friends of the Children-Portland: July 2014-July 2015*. Portland, OR: NPC Research.

Today, after two decades spent refining and improving the model, Friends of the Children is taking the big steps required to make a noticeable difference in the nation. New projects like the one in Tampa Bay are working exclusively with children in the foster care system. Along with Eckerd Kids, its partner organization, Friends of the Children started in Florida with more Friends and more children than any other Friends chapter.

***

ADD AN EXTRA ZERO to the annual Friends of the Children budget, and there could be fifty more programs at work in the nation. Add two more zeros, and Friends of the Children could be working with 140,000 children. Add a third zero—boosting the annual budget to $10 billion—and 1.4 million of the country's most at-risk children would have a Friend dedicating themselves and their time to their transformation. How's that for putting a dent in the 2.2 million children in poverty?

That kind of impact is years away, but Friends of the Children is okay with taking the small steps required when aiming for the best destinations. Week by week, child by child, Friends of the Children will get there no matter what.

Back at that fancy awards ceremony, where Duncan stood up on the stage wearing his tux looking out at a room full of people, he briefly mentioned a letter he received.

It was from one of the children who had been enrolled in the program, and though he only had time to read a few lines from it as he stood at the podium, there's just enough space left on these pages to share it with you in full.

Before you start, though, think about this: Though the letter is addressed to Duncan, it's really an open letter to anyone who will listen. It's to every Friend and every team member, every supporter and every champion. And if this book has stirred within you a desire to join with us and do something to help, then it is also a letter to you.

Dear Duncan,

Please allow me a moment to introduce myself. My name is Sofia Rodriguez, though I prefer to be called Noonie. I am a child currently enrolled in the Friends of the Children program. I have been involved in this organization for about ten years, and in that time I have been blessed with three exceptional Friends, as well as countless opportunities to meet amazing individuals. At this time I would like to offer you my most sincere gratitude, and the deepest love I have to give. I know that without your ambition, vision, and drive I would not have been fortunate enough to have met many, if any, of these people.

It is hard for me to try to describe the appreciation I feel toward you, my Friends, and this entire organization. However, I do intend to try. It is my hope that by writing you this letter you will have had a glimpse into the impact and influence that this astounding program has had not only on my life or the lives of the other children in it, but the surrounding people it touches as well. It is my aim to show you, by explaining the involvement of each one of my Friends, the deep admiration and gratitude that I hold for you.

My first Friend was a young woman named Andrea, and though admittedly I don't recall her very clearly, she is still one of the first people that validated my thoughts and feelings. She was also one of the only people who introduced me to other children my own age, and to adults who appeared to care about me. Without her influence I would not have learned the skills to form a relationship with one of my closest friends. To be honest, that thought alone fills me with great sadness.

My second Friend is an extremely important person to me. Her name is Renee. I have to admit that there were hard times within our relationship. However, as is true for any interpersonal connection, we were able to work through it and form a bond made to last forever. I find it hard to express the true nature of the joy, love, and overall emotions that overcome me whenever I think about this wonderful person. Our bond is irreplaceable, and was planted in sturdy ground, despite the complications that sometimes arose. It's a tie that was given to us by your hand, and for that I will always be indebted to you. There were often times when it became clear that without Renee's steady presence and understanding, I never would have come this far. It is due to the depth of our bond that I was able to rest in the knowledge that she would always be beside me, to cry, laugh, and feel for me when I no longer had the courage to do so.

I hope you can see the love that I have for her, the love I have for you. You have given me so much, you have allowed me to meet this person and to share a history and future with her. You have proved to me that no matter how hard life might seem at times, as long as there are people who care about you, you can keep moving forward. Thank you for showing me how truly lucky I am to be surrounded by people like you and the other Friends in the program.

My third Friend is one whom I find equally important to me, despite not having known her very long. After all, the bond between two people cannot be determined by any length of time. Already she has affected my life and shaped my attitude toward it. Lilly Smith is truly an impressive person, and she has so many delightful qualities that they are hard to sum up with words. It's simply astounding to me how her simple yet kind words have touched me so deeply. The kind of words others take for granted, the lectures that others frown at or roll their eyes to, I cherish and cling to. There isn't a day that goes by when I am not thankful for having her in my life. The experiences that I have had with her, while limited, have been so rewarding that I would not trade them for the world.

The love and appreciation I have for Lilly and Renee extends further than that of mere mentor and child. It reaches a place far deeper than friends, and, in the simplest terms, I would call these people my family. It matters little to me whether they feel the exact same way toward me or not, because I know that on some level they too care about me.

In short I cannot thank you enough for all you've given me. I cannot tell you what it means to me that you have extended your hand and offered me a place in your dream. It is people like you, Renee, and Lilly who are a once in a lifetime blessing. The experience alone has been so thrilling and life-changing that just thinking about it is a gratifying feeling. Just being able to know that in the world there are people who still care, who exist and who are so extremely loving and caring, warms my heart. To know that a person as rare as any one of these could believe that I have value gives me the strength to continue. This in turn affects not only me, but the peers with whom I come into contact in my day to day routine. By my growth and change, by the compassion I have been installed with, these students have been touched and helped by the unseen hands of a program far greater than that of any other I've seen.

And so I offer you this one last thank you, Duncan, because without you, Lilly and Renee I would not be the person I am today. I would not have the courage to stand up for what I believe in or find my voice. I would not have the ability to pick myself up and continue living. It is in this sense that you have saved me, and I am eternally grateful for that. I hope that by offering you this piece of my heart, this piece of my grat-

itude, that you will see how truly thankful I am, and how amazing you are. You are one of my greatest heroes and I pray that someday I will be at least half as driven, as kind, and as wonderful as you are.

With all my love, respect, and care,
Noonie

AFTERWORD

by Terri Sorensen,
President, Friends of the Children

This is where you come in. Each year Friends of the Children has been in operation has brought new lessons and a deeper understanding of how to more effectively help children. Each child brings his own story, her own needs, and each Friend has brought his own skills, her own passions. Though we started small—too small to make a noticeable dent on the 2.2 million children living in extreme poverty—still, year by year, Friend by Friend, week by week, things changed for the better. One child at a time, Friends of the Children has proven that the cycle of generational poverty can be broken.

If these stories of Nicky and Elijah, of Robert, and Jazmin, and all the others have inspired you, if the idea of breaking generational poverty, or getting society a $7 return for every $1 spent has caught your imagination, I would like you to consider the invitation that follows:

Will you invest?

Friends of the Children has found the answer to the problem that has troubled society for years. The better-funded the program is, the greater the impact it can make.

Invest in our $25 million expansion campaign to reach more children, and be a part of long-term transformation that really works.

Will you talk about Friends of the Children?

Tell others about this book, buy more copies as a gift, and pass them around, share your favorite stories among your friends and colleagues. Become an advocate for our kids and join in with the thousands of others who are spreading the word about the model that works.

Will you get involved?

If Friends of the Children is in a city near you, then come in to meet the team and see for yourself how it all works. Volunteer your time as a tutor, a fundraiser, or as a champion who helps inspire others. And if there's not a program in your city but you think there should be, talk to your local politicians and business leaders about how it works, and encourage them to take the first steps toward establishing a new chapter.

Support us, talk about us, come and work with us; the invitation is open to all.

Donations can be sent to:
Friends of the Children-National
44 NE Morris Street
Portland, OR 97212

www. friendsofthechildren.org
email: info@friendsofthechildren.org
Twitter: @FriendsNational
phone: 503.281.6633

ABOUT THE AUTHOR

Duncan Campbell's passion for helping society's most vulnerable children grew from his own experience as a youth growing up in North Portland in a welfare family where both parents were alcoholics and his father was in prison twice. As a child, he attended Highland/Martin Luther King grade school and Jefferson High School. His challenging childhood experiences eventually inspired him to create a number of children's organizations, including: Youth Resources, the Children's Institute, and a nationally recognized mentoring organization, Friends of the Children. Friends of the Children hires full-time professional mentors called Friends who each work with eight seriously at-risk children. Friends of the Children makes a commitment to each child from the end of kindergarten through high school. "I was one of those children," Duncan says of the youth served by Friends of the Children. "I believe," says Duncan, "people have a responsibility to reach back and take care of other people who are less fortunate, who by no choice of their own, are in unfortunate circumstances."

Friends of the Children is recognized as a model mentoring program for seriously at-risk children throughout the country. The organization has served thousands of children. We are in multiple locations throughout the U.S. and in the U.K.

Early in his career, Duncan was employed as a child-care worker for juvenile offenders at the Donald Long Home in Portland and at the Skipworth Detention Home in Eugene, Oregon. He has worked on the Governor's Children Agenda, was Chairman of the Multnomah County Juvenile Services Commission, was a founding board member of Children First, and is a board member with the Thrive Foundation for Youth. In addition, he was a delegate to the President's Summit for America's Future, and has been a speaker at the White House for the Helping America's Youth Initiative. Duncan has won numerous awards, including the prestigious national Purpose Prize from Civic Ventures for his impact as a social entrepreneur and champion for children. He is one of 25 Legends in Mentoring in the U.S.